HUMAN

DRAMA

I0172853

Across the

curriculum

HUMAN
DRAMA Across the
curriculum

A SYSTEMS EDUCATIONAL PROPOSAL

JONATHAN FLETCHER, PHD

Denver

ST. MAXIMUS
SCRIPTORIUM

Published in the United States by
St. Maximus Scriptorium
14 Inverness Drive East, Suite F-160
Englewood, CO 80112
(303) 708-1632
www.stmaxscript.com

Human Drama Across the Curriculum. Copyright © 2012 by Jonathan
Fletcher. All rights reserved. Printed in the United States of America.
No part of this book may be used or reproduced in any manner
whatsoever without written permission except in the case of brief
quotations embodied in critical articles and reviews.

ISBN: 978-0-9838399-3-4

Library of Congress Cataloging-in-Publication Data is available upon
request.

Published in association with Samizdat Creative
samizdatcreative.com

To

Bob Muldoon

whose encouragement and input were critical to this project

Contents

Introduction

The following is a program proposal for the development of the next generation of college preparatory students who must be able to function more effectively in constantly changing environments requiring higher-level thinking skills. For many years, schools have seen the value of integrating a number of skills across the curriculum, e.g. reading across the curriculum, writing across the curriculum, and finally, media across the curriculum. The concept is that there are certain universal skills that must be developed to a high degree for students to be successful at successively higher educational levels. This universality of cognitive skills points toward a fundamental question: are there other such skills that can be explicitly and implicitly addressed in the next-generation curriculum?

In addition, there has been a recognition that our current educational system, with its inherent silos of intellectual content such as math, science, and literature, fail to inform students of the interrelatedness of these areas and therefore fail to yield the highest possible level of understanding of the true meaning and importance of these areas of study. In other words, the desire to offer a more integrated curriculum has been tantalizingly looming as a potentially fruitful opportunity without being fully explored, let alone implemented. The difficulty with implementing an integrated curriculum arises from the failure to develop a set of principles that could serve as an organizing structure. How in the world does one do it?

These two driving needs—that of exploring the development of high-level cognitive skills as well as the need to integrate what appear to most students and teachers as highly disparate disciplines—form the driving motivations for this proposal. The premise is that a curriculum stressing the *processes* of discovery and creativity rather than simply the *results* of these endeavors and at the same time showing the inherent relatedness of all the factors that influence those processes, whether they involve social, scientific, technological, economic, historic, or psychological forces, will go far in addressing these two compelling educational challenges. *Human Drama Across the Curriculum* (HDAC) is an attempt to realize the profound potential of students who are in drastic need of more than the short-term acquisition of facts and skills but are in need of understanding, context, meaning and the ability to address problems and issues that they have never seen before. They need an armory of cognitive weapons to attack a host of challenges. They need to be able to *think*.[1]

Schools, both private and public, that are preparing students for a college education, are often endowed with highly educated faculty and bright highly motivated students. Many of these students will go on to do graduate work in academic disciplines or in professional areas such as medicine, engineering, business and law. Thus, the general goal of such schools is to prepare students to function in these demanding educational environments. Such themes as analytical thinking, critical thinking, and creativity are often used

---

[1]   While the terms "cognition" and "cognitive" are clearly appropriate, I prefer, in general, to use the word "thinking" as an effort to keep the discussion grounded in very basic concepts.

to describe the kinds of abilities these students will need—in addition to a solid foundation of knowledge content and skills. Traditionally, the educational system has focused on content at the expense of more advanced thinking skills. It was assumed that essential thinking skills would naturally be acquired while students attained proficiency in the content of more inherently complex areas such as mathematics, literary comprehension and composition, as well as the sciences. In more advanced curricula, these essential thinking skills were often further developed in the processes of reading and writing *across the curriculum*. While there is a current trend of talking about the need for developing these skills, the challenge remains to develop more explicit curricular and extracurricular experiences that will foster these qualities.

While reading, writing, and the use of media have a strong impact on the *effectiveness* of the learning process, to date most educational institutions have not formally addressed major overhauls of the *content* of the learning process. In primary school curricula math skills are taught separately from literature and composition skills, science is taught as separate units from social studies units. In high school, mathematics is still taught by the math teacher, chemistry is still taught by the chemistry teacher, French is still taught by the French teacher, art is still taught by the art teacher, English is still taught by the English teacher, and history is still taught by the history teacher. Traditional textbooks stress content while offering little insight into the thinking processes that went into the development of that content. While we have seen the tremendous advantages of integrating reading, writing, and media across the curriculum, the next challenge is to discern whether there are some new opportunities that have yet to be explored in the areas of curricular content—ones that would considerably enhance the learning experience, and result in students who are able not only to function more effectively in the traditional disciplines, but also can develop a whole new skill set related to the processes of analytical, critical, and creative thinking.

The general assertion that forms the basis of this proposal is that we as educators, and consequently the students under our guidance, spend a disproportionate amount of time on the results of a creative process and far too little time on the creative process itself. How do we expect students to learn to think for themselves if we do not present them with the fascinatingly rich tapestry that is formed by the human drama behind the results of that drama? *Human Drama Across the Curriculum* proposes to plumb the depths of this untapped wellspring through the study of carefully crafted biographical materials that stress the analytical, critical, and creative thinking processes that form the background of all human accomplishment. The proposal will discuss not only the rationale for such a program and its benefits but also some specifics regarding its implementation from primary to post-secondary education. The proposal will, in addition, discuss the importance of interdisciplinary integration as an organizing framework for understanding the thinking processes elucidated in the human dramas being studied. The use of simple "systems" concepts will be shown to be an integral part of developing the thinking skills being addressed.

Thinking Processes

Before suggesting a specific possible avenue, we need to consider what it means to think analytically, critically, and creatively. *Analytical thinking* is the ability to take apart something in order to see the parts and how they interact to form the whole. In systems thinking this would be the process of defining the system and its characteristics (boundary, inputs, elements, attributes, relations, processes, and outputs). *Critical thinking* refers to a process of comparing and contrasting alternatives, while drawing conclusions regarding the implications—either positive or negative—of the alternatives. *Creative thinking* is the process of discerning something new. In systems thinking it is the process of generating alternatives by a process of drawing together elements, attributes, and relations of things that are already understood in a new way. We might say that the first is about understanding something *in itself*, the second is about understanding something in relation to *other things*, and the third is about understanding known things in relation to the possibility of an *entirely new thing*.

It is useful to see how each of these cognitive approaches can be manifested in isolation. For example, a chemical analyst is one who determines the chemical constituents found in something. It is at least possible to imagine, in this case, pure analysis acting without significant components of critical or creative thinking, although in reality an analyst who does not have these other dimensions is a limited contributor.

A literary critic could be thought of as one who stresses the assessment of literary works in comparison to others or in comparison to some standard. It is at least possible to imagine that the critical effort far outweighs any analytical or creative inclinations, although again, a critic who does not have these other dimensions is a limited contributor. Finally, a modern artist could be seen as someone who is functioning deeply in the creative realm, without the components of either analytical or critical thinking. While one might imagine someone functioning primarily in the creative realm, such as an abstract painter splashing paint on a huge canvas, one need only look at Leonardo da Vinci to see how analytical and critical thinking greatly inform the creative process. In reality, these three types of thinking necessarily augment each other.

Using this basic understanding, one simplistically might say that any problem-solving process (in its most general form "the problem" being any situation in which one wants or needs simply to get from point A to point B) usually involves first analytical thinking to describe the problem, creative thinking in order to generate alternative solutions, and then critical thinking to differentiate and choose between the alternatives. Each of these "stages" of the thinking process is recursive in that any one can inform the others and itself at any point. Thus the thinking process becomes a veritable symphony of analysis, creativity, and critical thinking as the human mind manifests the most remarkable aspect of being human—the ability to think on a number of different levels in a number of different modes. Where in the educational process do we see these forms of thinking manifest? What kinds of curricula offer the richest opportunity to engage in the full range of analytical, critical and creative processes? It is suggested here that it is precisely in the liberal arts that the student gets exposed to the broadest expression of these kinds of thinking processes. In light of this understanding, one compelling challenge regards clearly articulating the value of the liberal education in terms of analytical, creative, and critical thinking. (Henceforth, we will use the term "critical thinking" to include both analytical and creative thinking.)

The Liberal Arts in School and College

One might say that the college preparatory program in any school has the same objectives as the liberal arts college: students must be broadly educated and prepared with the content and thinking skills necessary to function at higher levels of productivity, so that, when they are offered a wide range of study opportunities in college or graduate school, they are prepared to move in a number of alternative directions. Students need a "liberal" education in order to "keep their options open." In this context, therefore, we should look at the rationale for the liberal arts and its role in developing thinking skills. Why should one who is studying philosophy be exposed to physics? Why should one who is studying chemistry be exposed to Shakespeare? Why should one studying psychology be exposed to geology? We somehow assume that there is a benefit to a broad education, but often have a hard time articulating exactly what that benefit is. We are impressed by an engineer who can quote Shakespeare or an American doctor who is fluent in Swahili, but are hard pressed to explain how this diversity informs his or her effectiveness. Is it possible to clarify the rationale for the liberal arts education? The assertion being made here is that "systems thinking" is precisely the explicit rationale we are seeking.

Systems Thinking

To start with, one should assert that all *meaning* comes from *context*—the richer the context, the clearer and broader the meaning. So the first challenge is to create a rich context for the pieces of educational content. A date, a data point, a word, a musical note are all "meaningless" without the context in which that information takes on meaning—a chronology, a graph, a story, or a symphony. But there are a wide variety of contexts: space, time, conceptual, causal, formal, and systemic—each having a number of possible variations. This last one, the systemic context, is of particular importance as a justification for the liberal arts or a broad college preparatory curriculum. The reason one might study a wide range of what may appear to be highly disparate subject areas is that in every discipline there are *embedded systems* that have the potential to inform other systems in completely different disciplines. In the simple terminology of "general systems theory," a system is defined as a set of *elements* (e.g. characters in a play, chemicals in a chemical reaction, or variables in an equation), a set of *attributes* (e.g. one person is highly spiritual while the other is a football player, one chemical is highly unstable while the other glows in the dark, or one variable is a rational number while the other is an imaginary number), and a set of *relations* between those elements (e.g. two people in love, two chemicals that cause an explosion when mixed, or $ax + 1/y = 32$) that fall within a certain *boundary* (e.g.

the play, the reaction vessel, the set of all possible points in a plane). Once we have defined the specific elements, attributes and relations of a specific system that falls within the boundary we have defined, such as a bicycle/rider/roadway/traffic system, then our challenge is to make our understanding of this specific system applicable to other systems that may look much different but, in fact, have much in common with the system under study. The way we do this is to "defocus" from the specifics as one might defocus from the image of an individual. In doing so we see general characteristics but are not distracted with irrelevant particulars. General systems theory does this by the process of creating a meta-language to describe the system—a language that is more abstract than the specialized language of the discipline in which the system normally resides. For example, in the tale of Little Red Riding Hood, Red Riding Hood becomes the protagonist and the big bad wolf becomes the antagonist, the dialogue between them might be called the "encoded error-ridden communication stream," and the edge of the forest might be the "system boundary." Once this meta-language is created (and there are many ways the parts of a system can be described so that they can be related to other systems), it is possible to see the correspondence of the known system to another apparently disparate system under study. For example, in international relations there is from some vantage point a protagonist, an antagonist and an encoded error-ridden communication stream. In biological evolution within a prescribed ecological boundary, we can identify a protagonist, an antagonist, and an encoded error-ridden communication stream. By seeing the correspondence between the systems and then mapping the elements, attributes, and relations of a well-known system to those of another lesser known system, a known system begins to inform our understanding of the new system under study. Two systems that can be mapped using the meta-language are said to be *isomorphic*—having the same form.

Another simple example might be a talk on bonding that I gave to a group of Sewanee[2] chemistry students. It was on the eve of a party weekend during which they were about to engage in a kind of personal bonding common in such intensive social experiences. The question being addressed was whether one could create a meta-language to describe the elements, attributes, and relations associated with chemical bonds (ionic, covalent, and metallic) and then see if that understanding might inform our understanding of social bonding. The chemical bonding concepts of *donation/recption*, *highly controlled sharing*, and *uncontrolled sharing* became the meta-language for the discussion of how healthy and unhealthy relationships are formed.

This systems methodology really is a formal approach to developing the ability to see and use metaphors and analogies in problem solving. Thus there could be systems of characters in Hamlet that might inform certain reaction systems in chemistry. There might be paleontological processes of species extinction that inform linguistic and/or cultural changes. There might be economic forces of supply and demand that inform psychological environments. In each of these areas, we will be challenged by a host of problems. Our ability to think critically will depend on our ability to *see connections* between areas that may not exhibit obvious similarities. The ones who have quivers of the most diverse arrows and know how to shoot them will be in a much better position to contribute to the problem-solving process. Such a process might

---

[2]   The University of the South, Sewanee, Tennessee.

involve dissecting the problem into its essential components, generating a number of pathways to possible solutions, and engaging in the process of critically evaluating the short and long-term implications of the possible solutions in order to make an informed decision of the best path to take.

While systems thinking might be the most powerful set of critical thinking tools, it should be asserted that the development of explicit curriculum components in this area would be quite ambitious and could create such a discontinuity from past teaching methodologies as to yield an unworkable solution. Consequently I am proposing a sequential approach that would gradually exploit the power of systems thinking while being part of a broader curricular evolutionary process. Let us be clear that the guiding principles are: 1) do no harm to the acquisition of essential *content*, and 2) yield a net addition of significant critical thinking tools that should place that content in a richer context, resulting in deeper understanding, retention, and fruit for further critical thinking.

Current Approaches to Content Education

While we might not delve too deeply into the abstract methodology of systems analysis in the college preparatory curriculum, it might be important to understand the possibilities inherent in a broad education and the many ways it can inform the process of critical thinking. With this in mind, we should consider the various ways in which this approach to the enhancement of critical thinking could take place. Of primary importance is the realization that we are suggesting a shift in focus from the development of information acquisition/expression tools (reading, writing, and media) across the curriculum (themselves essential parts of the critical thinking skill set) to a focus on the development of critical thinking tools within the way curricular content is chosen, explored, discussed, and otherwise presented. How might the traditional components of English, history, language arts, mathematics, fine arts, and science be reshaped to take full advantage of the possibilities for developing critical thinking skills? Certainly these disciplines, as they are usually taught in the college preparatory setting, inherently contain challenges for students to think critically. However, we will not understand the considerable enhanced possibilities until we offer some examples of how the status quo works. The following are some examples of traditional approaches.

To the extent that history is seen as a chronology of events and not as a human drama filled with people thinking critically, is precisely the degree to which our pedagogical approach falls short of its potential. Our textbook for freshman history at Sewanee— R. R. Palmer's *A History of the Modern World*—is a perfect example of the traditional way in which history is still taught. There is simply no way to cover such a broad scope, tapping into the essential human drama that has taken place, which had a profound impact on the results of history. Unfortunately, if we limit ourselves merely to the results of history and not to the processes, we fail to offer students vital examples of the kind of cognitive processes that are essential in understanding the historical process—any historical process.

To the extent that science is taught as a current state of the art and not as a human drama filled with people thinking critically, failing, stumbling, falling into ego traps, and exhibiting considerable courage to "buck the system," we fall far short of the potential to instruct in the very thinking processes that made the results possible. A perfect example of this problem is the current process of publishing juried scientific journals. Journal articles are concise descriptions of the *results* of science, but not the *process* of science. What students who are developing critical thinking tools really need are not just the results, but a detailed description of the ebb and flow of hopes, dreams, failures, and modest successes, all of which might seem to most of us as merely a trivial experience related to a significant breakthrough. It is these often undisclosed moments that shine like a beacon, drawing the scientist on to further discovery. (An analogy might be the way a rare birdie putt draws a golfer to continued effort or a rare homerun lights up a batter's vision of the possible.)

To the extent that languages and literature are taught as givens and not as a part of a process of human critical thinking, we fall short of the possibilities. Faulkner's novels cannot be fully appreciated independent of his life. Shakespeare's plays cannot be appreciated independent of the context in which they were written. But here is the rub. *How do we articulate that context in such a way as to fully explore the possibilities for informing critical thinking?* The only way to do this is to show how critical thinking played a role in the life of the author—in the process of producing the final result. How do writers write? On what do they draw? Faulkner, for example, drew on a much narrower set of source materials than Hemingway without sacrificing richness. Faulkner was fully satisfied with his narrow local environment. On the other hand, Hemingway was driven frenetically toward new experiences—a drive that may have considerably contributed to his late stage of angst and final suicide. *To the extent that we do not deal with this human drama is precisely the degree to which we strip the results of the context of the creative process out of which those results arose.*

To the extent that we teach mathematics as a set of skills to solve quantitative problems and not as the product of a compelling process of trial and error, even human struggle, we have lopped off the most tantalizing part of the steak. We have thrown away the tenderloin. What did Archimedes know and when did he know it? How daring was the leap from finite geometric solutions of Euclid to the infinitesimal thinking of Archimedes that laid the groundwork for calculus 1800 years later? How did the civil responsibilities of mathematicians such as Monge, Leibniz, and Newton influence the scope of their thinking? How did the scientific interests of mathematicians such as Pascal and Newton inform the development of their mathematical tools? If we do not address such questions, how can we as students and teachers hope to grow as critical thinkers as well as technical mathematicians?

The Great Books Curriculum

Before we forge ahead with the general theme of this proposal, we should pause to consider the Great Books Curriculum (GBC) of St. John's College in Annapolis, Maryland and Santa Fe, New Mexico. Developed in the 1930s, the curriculum, designed by Scott Buchannan and Stringfellow Barr in collaboration with a number of folks at the University of Chicago, was founded on the belief that students would be much better served by reading, studying, and discussing the greatest works of literature, philosophy, science, and mathematics in their original form rather than studying textbooks that have distilled the results of these great authors into logical and much more pedagogically tight textbooks. Because of the highly integrated nature of the GBC, tutors who eventually were expected to be conversant in all the works in the curriculum, replaced professors who were highly specialized in their respective disciplines. Because the tutors were models of integrated knowledge and were involved intimately with the discussion of all the works in the curriculum, students were exposed to critical thinking not only in the context of the works themselves, but also in the exposure to the thinking of the tutors. A further integration of the curriculum took place in the fact that all students read all the same books. Thus, intellectual discussion within the college community was facilitated by the common experiences of the students and tutors at any given time.

The limitation with this approach is that, for example, one learns little of Euclid's critical thinking by reading his *Elements*. Again, this is an exploration of results and not of process. By working one's way through Euclid's proofs, one certainly gains analytical skills, but the learning is highly skewed toward geometry for its own sake, speaking little to the broader objectives of the liberal education. But what if we could study Euclid's development as a geometer? What did he know and when did he know it? What if we could see his struggles, his failures, his eureka moments? Sometimes this is possible by reading the results of an author. Augustine's *Confessions*, Descartes' *Discourse on the Method*, and Faraday's *Experimental Researches in Electricity* offer much of this kind of material, but a biographer who has access not only to these but other materials—such as opinions of others, correspondence, and diaries—can give a much fuller account of the operative processes—the *human drama*. It is not so much that the GBC is not a remarkably integrated curriculum to be greatly admired. The question is whether there is some aspect of the curriculum that could be made more explicit, offering students a greater set of thinking tools. Where St. John's says that the GBC is about *ideas*, I would say that the curriculum I am proposing is about *thinking*. The former is about *results*. The latter is about *process*. Each of these curricula concerns itself with both of these concepts. The emphasis in the curriculum being proposed here, however, may be somewhat different than that in the GBC and certainly more explicit.

While treated only implicitly in the GBC, systems thinking would be treated much more explicitly and deliberately in this curriculum. Although the studying and discussing of the Great Books offers infinite possibilities for discerning connections between the broad range of ideas to which students are being exposed, formal tools for engaging in higher levels of analytical, critical, and creative thinking may be missing. Systems approaches have the power to turn implicit connections into explicit isomorphic systems.

Choosing an Approach

Let us lay out a number of possibilities that might represent some sort of universe to aid in the decision-making context. These might include:

1. History across the curriculum
2. Mathematics across the curriculum
3. Economics across the curriculum
4. Science across the curriculum
5. Philosophy across the curriculum
6. System Analysis across the curriculum

One might assert that a fully integrated curriculum would be an expression of all of these possibilities. The challenge is to decide on how to start. How would one go about deciding on a starting point among these possibilities, describing how the evolutionary process might take place, what the goals of the process might be, and what the results of the process might be? As one can see, these projects are successively more challenging. To decide on the starting point, the first question might be to consider the words "across the curriculum." What are we trying to accomplish by doing anything "across the curriculum?" We are looking for some universal principles from one discipline that apply to all disciplines. In this regard one might assert that all disciplines have a history and have evolved through time. All disciplines have quantitative issues that have posed challenges and have required either simple or complex mathematics to inform the development of the discipline. All disciplines exhibit some form of tension between that which is available and that which is desired. In other words, there is an economy involved in every discipline. If science involves the processes of induction and deduction, one could assert that all disciplines exhibit science in some form.[3] All disciplines are founded on conceptual bases that have roots in areas traditionally reserved for philosophy—ethics, morals, epistemology, ontology, teleology, etc. To see how these issues are implicitly or explicitly dealt with in every discipline would be a powerful form of integration. And of course, systems theory is the great integrator.

The most straightforward application might be the first, since all human endeavor takes place in time and space—in other words in history. Thus it makes sense to start here with any effort to integrate content across the curriculum. Unfortunately, many would assert that we already look at the history of science, math, literature, etc. at some level. The challenge, however, would be to drive the curriculum away from simple chronology toward the processes of critical thinking that formed the foundation of each historical result. If we can do this, we may have found our doorway into a new dimension of cognitive education.

Let us consider one general tendency—that of the increased interest among adults to read biographies. As we get older, why do our reading tastes shift away from mere history to biographies of those who were key participants in that history? Why are we fascinated by the stories of how

---

[3]   In fact it is precisely the search for more "scientific" approaches in the less quantifiable disciplines that has led to considerable strides in theory often leading to disastrous results, e.g. the quantification of complex markets leading to trading models that ignore the increased correlation of trading decisions resulting in significant market instability.

Bill Gates built Microsoft or how Steve Jobs overcame both personal and logistical challenges to build Apple? Why are we still captivated by the stories surrounding those who were instrumental in the founding of our country such as Washington, Jefferson or Andrew Jackson. Or those, who for good or ill, formed our modern international relationships such as Franklin Roosevelt, Winston Churchill, Adolph Hitler, and Joseph Stalin. Why are we enthralled by the struggles of Michelangelo or Van Gogh? No matter what we as individuals see as a vision for our own lives, we can find parallels in the lives of others. We do not find those parallels in historical chronologies, mathematical equations or scientific theories. We find them in the human dramas of people who struggled with the same things we do. Their human dramas are like our human dramas. To the extent that we can see and appreciate their drama is precisely the degree to which that drama might inform ours. If they could do it, just maybe I can do it. If I can see the analytical, critical and creative thinking processes that allowed them to triumph over challenges and adversity, I can use that same kind of thinking to overcome my own challenges and adversity.

Consequently, we are now convinced of our educational pathway. We will use biography as an access point to the human dramas of individuals which in turn will give us access to the analytical, critical and creative thinking that allowed them to be successful—and we will do this in every discipline—history, math, science, economics, psychology, etc. We will do this "across the curriculum," and in so doing show how within the human drama of one person all of the disciplines interact to create the stage on which each drama is acted out. This is why we are calling the effort "Human Drama Across the Curriculum." It is within this human drama, which forms the backdrop of all human accomplishment, that we will discern analytical, creative, and critical thinking.

The first prejudice to be overcome, however, would be the traditional understanding of history as being some form of simplistic time line of events with rudimentary cause and effect relationships. For example:

1. The First World War was triggered as a result of the assassination of the Archduke Franz Ferdinand of Austria in Sarajevo on June 28, 1914.
2. The Great Depression began on "Black Tuesday" with the Wall Street Crash of October, 1929.
3. Radium was discovered by Pierre and Marie Curie in 1898.
4. The fall of the Berlin Wall on November 9, 1989 was an integral part of the collapse of the Soviet Union that was completed by the seizure of power by Boris Yeltsin in 1991.

It is not that these are false or misleading statements. The problem is that only a small number of students of these events are in a position to understand the significance of the carefully chosen wording. What we end up with as students is a collection of timeline elements and rudimentary cause-and-effect relationships that offer us few paradigms that can be used in other situations to aid in our critical thinking. By "Human Drama Across the Curriculum" we do not imply that we would introduce even more such historic elements. While it is clearly an historical perspective, we should look more carefully at the value of such a perspective and try to extract an approach that will offer the student a deeper appreciation of the events that are thus placed in this historical context. The essential perspective of this proposal is this:

critical thinking is always done by people within some historic context. The response of world leaders to the series of
events that led to WWI involves critical thinking by individuals with or without the power base to make those responses
felt. For we as students of history to use history as a resource
to inform our own critical thinking, we must delve below
the surface of the actors in history to discover their own
critical thinking. Unfortunately, the way events are reported,
the cognitive processes are usually obscured in favor of the
results. No one is interested in failures (except maybe Hitler's
failure at Stalingrad), although it is the failures that are at
least as important as the successes in elucidating the critical
thinking process. News stories tell what happened—at least
at first. Scientific journals report on results, not the hurley-
burley processes that often led to those results. Thinking is
dirty business, and we, as educators, are often bound and
determined to clean it up. We, as teachers, love to present
"demonstrations" but shrink from performing experiments
when we are unsure of the results. What if it does not work?
So we try it out before class. When we do this, however, we
unwittingly throw out the thinking baby with the bathwater.

Creativity often involves a certain amount of serendipity.
Thomas Edison knew that he often needed to try thousands
of possible approaches before he stumbled upon something
that showed a glimmer of possibility. All critical thinking involves a certain amount of failure and wheel-spinning. If we
are to teach students about critical thinking we must model the process in two ways: first, we must talk about others'
thinking processes to the extent to which we can uncov-
er them, and second, we must model that open-ended process in which things often do not work. To do this we must
get below the surface of history textbooks and look at the

contexts in which these historical figures had to engage in critical thinking. We need to use *biography* as the foundation of any program in "Human Drama Across the Curriculum." Furthermore we need to seek the type of biographies in which the author pursues the mindset of the protagonist, exposing his or her critical thinking processes. Because thinking processes are difficult to reveal completely, there are two pieces of information that we must look for before we can hope to fill in the blanks: first, *What did he or she know?* And second, *When did he or she know it?* (Note: We will henceforth refer to the "Human Drama Across the Curriculum" program as the "Human Drama Curriculum" or HDC.)

An Integrated Educational Program

The great advantage of a college preparatory curriculum that involves grades K through 12 is that one can be deliberate in integrating the curriculum. There are three areas that come to mind as opportunities in this regard:

1. Explicitly building on the prior year's concepts through the use of materials that are familiar to the student, but exhibit additional aspects that reflect a higher level of complexity.

2. Building on the same biographical subjects at successively higher levels of complexity and understanding.

3. Building on an ever-growing inventory of systems concepts that allow the student to function at successively more complex levels of analytical, critical, and creative thinking, thus addressing the *same problems* (e.g. the nature of light) at successively higher levels of complexity.

Any integrated educational program is essentially cumulative. Each successive year sees the addition of new knowledge in the context of all previously learned knowledge. If one is to learn something about Newton, for example, then by the time one graduates, one should have been exposed to Newton at least 5 or 6 times with the same basic information repeated many times. These basic pieces of information comprise the compass points of his life that allow the student to quickly place him in the historical and conceptual context in which his life takes on meaning. Dates are important, but not as an end in themselves. Nationality and education are important, but not as ends in themselves. Ultimately one would like to have a tight framework in which to see the *human drama* played out in order to appreciate the amazing leaps of analytical, critical, and creative thinking that have led to major human accomplishment.

This proposal relates to the continuation of a process that has already begun at many schools and colleges but can be carried to levels of integration that most curricula never approach. As we move forward, we will assume the ultimate goal of a highly integrated curriculum.

Human Drama Curriculum in Perspective

There are two issues that need to be addressed in understanding the value of human drama in any curriculum: the first is pedagogical, while the second is philosophical. Our first assertion is that one learns the results of any process by appreciating and to some extent participating in the process. We do this by studying the thinking processes of others through their biographies. We have addressed this aspect of the curriculum above. The second is a bit more subtle and controversial. The question might be posed this way—*why study the great achievers at all?* Why not just study the great pool of results? Do great people count?

The idea that history is driven by the contributions of great people is often associated with the work of Thomas Carlyle. The following quotation captures some of what has been called the "great man" theory of history:[4]

> We have undertaken to discourse here for a little on Great Men, their manner of appearance in our world's business, how they have shaped themselves in the world's history, what ideas men formed of them, what work they did;—on

---

[4] Note: We do recognize the inherent limitations of the male-centered vocabulary reflective of the times in which the following authors wrote, but we are stuck with it. As you will see from the list of great people, it is replete with great women.

Heroes, namely, and on their reception and per-
formance; what I call Hero-worship and the Heroic in human affairs....For, as I take it, Universal
History, the history of what man has accomplished in this world, is at bottom the History
of the Great Man [or Great Woman] who have
worked here. They were the leaders of men, these
great ones; the modelers, patterns, and in a side
sense creators, of whatsoever the general mass of
men contrived to do or to attain; all things that
we see standing accomplished in the world are
properly the outer material result, the practical
realization and embodiment, of Thoughts that
dwelt in the Great Men sent into the world: the
soul of the whole world's history, it may justly be
considered, were the history of these.[5]

William James was a proponent of the "great man" theory
of history as indicated by the following:

The causes of production of great men lie in a
sphere wholly inaccessible to the social philosopher. He must simply accept geniuses as data, just
as Darwin accepts his spontaneous variations. For
him, as for Darwin, the only problem is, these
data being given, How does the environment
affect them, and how do they affect the environment? Now, I affirm that the relation of the
visible environment to the great man is in the
main exactly what it is to the "variation" in the

---

[5]   Thomas Carlyle, *Heroes, Hero-worship, and the Heroic in History*
(John Wiley, 1861), 2.

Darwinian philosophy. It chiefly adopts or re-
jects, preserves or destroys, in short selects him.
And whenever it adopts and preserves the great
man, it becomes modified by his influence in an
entirely original and peculiar way. He acts as a
ferment, and changes its constitution, just as the
advent of a new zoological species changes the
faunal and floral equilibrium of the region in
which it appears.[6]

John Stuart Mill expressed his support for the theory in
the following quotation:

I believe that if Newton had not lived, the world
must have waited for the Newtonian philosophy until there had been another Newton or his
equivalent. No ordinary man, and no succession
of ordinary men, could have achieved it. I will
not go the length of saying that what Newton
did in a single life might not have been done in
successive steps by some of those who followed
him each singly inferior to him in genius. But
even the least of those steps required a man of
great intellectual superiority.[7]

Finally let us consider historical concepts found in the
work of Georg Wilhelm Friedrich Hegel.

---

[6]   William James, "Great Men, Great Thoughts, and the Environment," Atlantic Monthly, 1880.
[7]   Robert L. Carneiro, *The Muse of History and the Science of Culture*
(New York: Springer, 2000), 114.

[His work,] *The Philosophy of History* remains at the heart and center of Hegel's philosophy... For Hegel's whole philosophy is historically conceived...All his basic notions, such as the world spirit, reason, freedom, receive their meaning and significance within a historical context... He was putting forward a philosophical framework for history... he was not writing history, but philosophy.[8]

History is seen as the march of [human] freedom through the world. This march of freedom is interpreted as what the World Spirit wants, as it seeks to realize itself. And in its effort to realize itself, it employs people, world-historical peoples to do its work.[9]

What Hegel is manifestly talking about is the great cultures or civilizations...If we read the extraordinary pages in which Hegel testifies to the complete change that came into the world with the coming of Christ, we cannot but realize that these great cultures, put to work by the world spirit in its effort to realize itself, are radically affected by *the action of one being*, which revolutionized history so that it was never the same afterward.[10]

---

[8]   G. W. F Hegel, *The Philosophy of History* (Dover Books, 1956), Introduction by Professor C. J. Friedrich, Harvard University, p. 1.

[9]   *Ibid.*, p. 2.

[10]   *Ibid.*, p. 3.

We should note that the Great Man theory of history has not been universally accepted. Herbert Spencer and many others were critical of the theory for its dependence on conditions that did not lend themselves to systematic and scientific study. If the major events of history are controlled by the fortuitous interventions of improbable human activities, then what can historians study? If we can find no cause and effect relationships in history then we are certainly doomed to repeat it. In *The Study of Sociology*, written in 1782, Spencer said the following:

> If it be a fact that the great man may modify his nation in its structure and actions, it is also a fact that there must have been those antecedent modifications constituting national progress before he could be evolved. Before he can re-make his society, his society must make him. So that all those changes of which he is the proximate initiator have their chief causes in the generations he descended from. If there is to be anything like a real explanation of these changes, it must be sought in that aggregate of conditions out of which both he and they have arisen.[11]

Taking a similar position, R. G. Collingwood wrote in his 1946 work, *The Idea of History*:

> Of everything other than thought, there can be no history. Thus a biography, for example, however much history it contains, is constructed on principles that are not only non-historical but

---

[11]   Carneiro, p. 115.

anti-historical. Its limits are biological events, the birth and death of a human organism: its framework is thus a framework not of thought but of natural process. Through this framework—the bodily life of the man, with his childhood, maturity and senescence, his diseases and all the accidents of animal existence—the tides of thought, his own and others', flow crosswise, regardless of its structure, like sea-water through a stranded wreck. Many human emotions are bound up with the spectacle of such bodily life in its vicissitudes, and biography, as a form of literature, feeds these emotions and may give them wholesome food; but this is not history.[12]

As is often the case, the problem is one of emphasis. Adherents to a position often err on the side of exclusivity and fail to take into account the activity of multiple forces. Certainly great personages are formed by the circumstances in which they find themselves. In the HDC, this is precisely one of the reasons we study these individuals, *to get a clearer picture of the cultures that formed them.* It is equally true that individuals often use the resources and cultures available to them in vastly different ways, some creating remarkable contributions that others are unable to make. A 2007 *New York Times* bestseller, *The Black Swan*, points out the folly of trying to do history "scientifically." Financial markets adhere, at least to some extent, to a "random walk" principle with secular trends due to normal market forces that are periodically overwhelmed by major unforeseeable events ("black

---

[12]   R. G. Collingwood, *The Idea of History* (Galaxy Books – Oxford University Press, 1956), p. 304.

swans"—events that should not occur according to any rea-
sonable analysis *of the past*).[13] With this same possibility in
mind, the "great man" theory in its best form should assume
a cultural milieu out of which arises a human "black swan"
who instigates an entire paradigm shift (such as Isaac Newton
in mechanics and Albert Einstein in relativity theory).

In other words, this discussion of the philosophical backdrop for studying the lives of great contributors simply points
out that the validity of such study has been a heated topic
for hundreds of years. We submit that this debate, while it
informs the present proposal, does not form in any way a
sine qua non that makes or breaks the case for the present curriculum additions. As the HDC program proceeds, there is
no doubt that insight will be gained as to how the program
might best be put to use within the larger context of the
overall curriculum. It may be that, just as "media" became
the subject of its own study, the HDC may become the subject of its own dialogue appropriate to the grade levels in
which it is being introduced.

---

[13]   Nassim Taleb, *The Black Swan* (New York: Random House,
2007), p. xvii-xxviii.

I Don't Know, Let's Try It

One of the methodologies that seems to follow directly from the concept of Human Drama Across the Curriculum is the idea of entering into the human drama by engaging in the same analytical, critical and creative thinking processes: Encouraging the students to try things out without any particular expectation of success or failure, but merely the joy of inquiry. One example of this process was a laboratory I taught to college students in a course entitled "Contemporary Earth Science" at Benedict College in Columbia, South Carolina. The lab was an open-ended experience of making iron—from scratch. The students were told that if they could whip up a batch of iron, they could skip the lab. Short of that, we would start at the beginning and learn how to make fire. The class was divided into groups of four students each. They were given a set of directions for making fire from an old woodcraft handbook and told to gather the needed materials for the next lab in a week. When they arrived at lab the following week they were told to get busy and follow the directions. A full description of the fascinating pedagogical exercise is beyond the scope of this discussion, but some key features are important. The students struggled to understand just exactly what the directions and pictures meant as they tried to translate them into a practical application. They would ask whether they should do this or that, and I would respond, "Try it." After a while they learned that they would get no answers from the teacher. Amidst the cacophony of the lab with five groups all talking and working at the same time, the sound of one phase arose over all the noise, "I don't know, let's try it."

The application of critical thinking is predicated on the premise that the willingness and desire to "try it" is central to the teaching and learning processes. The teacher becomes a cheerleader and maybe a subtle guide. In one instance a girl came up with a good idea, and I simply said, "Why don't you let her lead the group for a while." As one watched the groups make progress by making a series of silly mistakes, one was struck by the high level of ownership each student and group took over the results of their struggle. When the class finally tried to demonstrate how far they had gotten, the project was functionally a failure. No one had actually made fire. They had made a lot of smoke, but never got just the right conditions actually to get a flame. While the project objective appeared to be *making* fire, in reality it was to *try* to make fire, and from that perspective the project was a raving success.

I should give you the punch line. We made a bellows and charcoal, obtained limestone and iron ore put it in a small pit and cooked the bejabbers out of the mixture. The result was a jagged brown chunk of something. One day I was sitting in my office looking at this nondescript piece of material when in walked a history professor, Ashby Morton. "Ashby, I am not sure what I have here, do you have any ideas?" "Well," he said, "do you have a magnet?" I reached into the bottom drawer of my desk and brought out a powerful permanent magnet. Thunk! We both started to laugh. "Well, bless my soul—IRON!" It was a bit scruffy, but unquestionably the real McCoy.

Another incident may serve to reinforce the point. I was teaching a summer course for teachers entitled "Interdisciplinary Science for Teachers." The course was an opportunity to show primary and secondary school teachers something about using the broad scope of the sciences to solve problems. The subject area we chose was the water cycle—precipitation, transpiration, evaporation, condensation, and back to precipitation. We chose a specific area on the map as our study area and the teachers were asked to design and carry out an experiment to quantify some aspect of the water cycle in the study area. The question was, how much water was involved in these various processes over a given area over a period of a year? Remember, these teachers were used to doing demonstrations but had little experience with the open-ended nature of true experimentation. I asked them to keep a journal of each day's activities and particularly their thinking processes. The stunning thing about the whole process seen in each student's journal entries was the ebb and flow of emotions. They began with confidence and enthusiasm as they designed their particular experiments. This was followed by a period of frustration as they began to realize that their experiment would not work as planned or did not yield the information necessary to address the problem they had chosen. This was followed by gradual progress and a lifting of spirits which in many cases was followed by a high level of satisfaction once they had put all the pieces of their puzzle together and could make some kind of informed statement concerning their area of interest. Once we put all this information together and realized just what a complex task we had been addressing, the teachers (I hope) received a better understanding of the analytical, critical and creative processes associated with addressing any scientific question.

To the degree that we, as teachers, strip away this struggle and the concomitant joy of overcoming challenges is precisely the degree that we rob our students of any kind of understanding of the creative process. Scientists, writers, engineers, doctors, lawyers, and even Indian chiefs, if they are any good, are not in the game to repeat "demonstrations" but are in the game to solve problems, overcome obstacles and figure things out. One inherent aspect of problem solving is failure, analysis, comparison, creating a new approach, and trying again. The mantra "I don't know, let's try it" is the universal call to the joys of thinking and finding answers. As we study the human drama of those who went before us, thinking and finding answers, we gain great insights into our own progress along the same creative pathways.

Some Examples of the Human Drama Curriculum

Before we get into more detail concerning just what we mean by this process, let us outline some specific examples of how this might work across the curriculum. Consider the following four traditional areas of study: science, mathematics, literature, and history. Because we are dependent on the biographer to translate the words of the subject as well as to interpret the meaning of the pieces of available information, we are essentially listening to the voice of the biographer. For this reason, we will be using numerous quotations below to indicate the richness that is available in a good biography. The biographies become the data sources for our study, and consequently become the object of study themselves. Teaching students to view a biography critically is all part of the HDC. Finally, we should comment that all quotations are given as originally written by their respective authors as transmitted by the biographer, with minimal corrections. We are indicating what the biographer wrote, and usually the biographer is trying to be true to what the subject wrote—mistakes and all.

Human Drama in the Sciences - Michael Faraday
One of the most interesting examples of this approach is the

study of science. Science is all about the process of discovery, and, therefore, is about the process of failure. We are betrayed at every turn because our textbooks and journals merely present the results of what is often a tortuous and fascinating process. Consider, for example, the discovery of electrical induction by Michael Faraday. L. Pearce Williams has written a wonderful biography of Faraday, which takes a decidedly scientific approach. In his chapter entitled "The Discovery of Electromagnetic Induction," he goes into considerable detail about what Faraday knew, when he knew it, and what experiments he did to bridge the gap between the state of the art and his extension of that state.

First, let us consider Faraday's background, which sets the stage for his accomplishment in the areas of chemistry and electromagnetism. Michael Faraday was born into a modest household in 1791. He lacked any formal education, but was influenced strongly in two ways: first, his association with the Sandemanian Christian sect, and second, his work as an apprentice to a bookbinder. In the first case, the influence can be indicated by an entry of a friend's diary and Williams' following comment:

> 'I think that a good deal of Faraday's week-day strength and persistency might be referred to his Sunday Exercises. He drinks from a fount on Sunday which refreshes his soul for the week.' Serene, kind, ascetic and anti-social: these Faraday certainly was. How many of these characteristics he owed to his religion it is impossible to say, but certainly any natural tendencies towards them were stimulated by his religious training.[14]

---

[14]   L. Pearce Williams, *Michael Faraday* (Chapman and Hall, 1965), p. 6.

The second influence is multifaceted. Because of his economic station, Faraday was apprenticed to a bookbinder when he was 14. This was the first of many fortuitous conditions in which he found himself for various reasons. First, the manual labor associated with book binding suited and enhanced his natural inclination toward the sensory aspects of his thirst for knowledge. He was always the supreme experimenter, and his theoretical skills were always tied to the physical expression of some phenomenon. He was an arch empiricist—always relying on the doing and first-hand experience. Other livelihoods would not have reinforced this tendency and natural curiosity as well as book binding, which involved precise physical work as well as an exposure to a number of materials and substances used in the trade. Second, he was exposed to a wide array of books that were sent in for binding. This exposure was of monumental importance in allowing his thirsty mind to wade into a highly diverse river of knowledge. Finally, his master was himself a widely read intellect and encouraged Faraday not only by lending him books from his own library, but also allowing him to use space in the back of the shop to set up a primitive laboratory in which he could begin to develop his experimental inclinations and skills. Faraday himself acknowledges his attitude toward his master and the opportunity his work there afforded him:

> Sir
> When first I evinced a predilection for the sciences but more particularly for that one denominated electricity you kindly interested yourself in the progress I made in the knowledge of facts relating to the different theories in existence

readily permitting me to examine those books in
your possession that were any way related to the
subjects then occupying my attention. To you,
therefore, is to be attributed the rise and existence of that small portion of knowledge relating
to the sciences which I possess and accordingly to
you are due my acknowledgements.[15]

The following notes from his master and Williams' comments further enhance this picture:

'…after the regular hours of Business, he was
chiefly employed in Drawing and Copying from
the Artists Repository a work published in Num-
bers which he took in weekly – also Electrical
Machines from the Dicty. Of Arts and Sciences and other works which came in to bind… he
went an early walk in the Morning Visiting always some Works of Art or searching for some
Mineral or Vegetable curiosity – Holloway Water
Works, Highgate Archway, W Middlesex Water
Works – Strand Bridge – Junction Water Works
etc. etc. …his mind ever engaged, besides at-
tending to Bookbinding which he executed in a
proper manner…

If I had any curious book from my Customers
to bind, with Plates, he would copy such as he
thought Singular or Clever, which I advised him
to Keep by him. Irelands Hogarth, and other
Graphic Works, he much admired [Thompson's]

[15]   *Ibid.*, p. 10.

Chemistry in 4 vols. he bought and interleaved great part of it, Occasionally adding Notes with Drawings and Observations.' There is a note of frenzy about this activity. Copying, drawing, noting, exploring but to what end? Where was the unifying thread that could bind these isolated and insulated facts together?[16]

Thus, his work gave Faraday access to knowledge, but as Williams points out, knowledge that is self-acquired often lacks a certain discipline. The answer was to be found in a book by Isaac Watts, entitled *The Improvement of the Mind*. This single work, discovered in the bookbindery, was the most formative organizing force for Faraday's intellectual development. Of the many prescriptions Watts offers, all of which Faraday took to heart, the one that is most telling of his industry and ambition was the admonition to write letters. Watts talks of this endeavor as one of salutary use in the development of one's mind. Faraday wrote the following letter to a friend:

I speak not of the abuse but the use of epistolation (if you will allow me to coin a new word to express myself) and that use, I have no doubt, produces other good effects. Now I do not profess myself perfect in those points, and my deficiency in others connected with the subject you well know, as grammar, &c.; therefore it follows that I want improving on these points; and what so natural in a disease as to revert to the remedy that will perform a cure? and more so when the

---

[16]   *Ibid.*, p. 11.

physic is so pleasant; or, to express it in a more
logical manner and consequently more philo-
sophically, M. F. is deficient in certain points that
he wants to make up, epistolary writing is one
cure for those deficiencies, therefore, I should
practice epistolary writing.[17]

The bindery led to his involvement with the City Philosophical Society and finally to his good fortune to meet
someone who could get him a ticket to lectures by Sir
Humphry Davy at the Royal Institution. This exposure and
access to the height of scientific investigation led Faraday to
the conclusion that his future lay in research. When he fin-
ished his apprenticeship, Faraday immediately tried to devise
a plan whereby he might pursue his dream. How this took
place is a fascinating story of human drama. The turning
point came when one of the apprentices at the Royal Institution was dismissed for brawling. Davy offered Faraday the
appointment and he accepted. "The minutes of the meeting
of the Managers of the Royal Institution for 1 March 1813
read: 'Resolved – that Michael Faraday be engaged to fill the
situation lately occupied by Mr. Payne on the same terms'.
Faraday had finally entered the Temple."[18]

While the story of Faraday's intellectual development is
important, it is equally important to show how this intellect
was engaged in pressing the bounds of science. We now turn
to one of the most stunning examples of his mind at work in
the discovery of electromagnetic induction. Here we are in-
debted greatly to Williams for his desire to expose the details
of Faraday's thinking processes. The following quotation sets
the stage.

---

[17]   *Ibid.*, p. 21.
[18]   *Ibid.*, p. 29

After 1821 Faraday's mind was occupied by a host
of other problems and his time was too filled
with other duties to permit him to bring his full
attention to bear on electromagnetism.[19]

Does critical thinking have anything to do with distractions?

If we are to understand Faraday's mental evolution, both before and after 1831, the development
of his ideas on the nature of electricity and the
reasons behind his famous ring experiment must
be seen as clearly as possible.[20]

Here Williams is directly addressing the theme of the Human Drama Curriculum. This is precisely the point. *The reasons behind* are what we need to discover if we are not only
to understand the event in all its fullness, but also if we are
to use that understanding in addressing challenges that we
ourselves face. *The reasons behind* are what is missing and *the
reasons behind* are what we are about in the HDC.

Let us set the scientific stage further. In the winter of 1819
Hans Christian Oersted set up a simple experiment:

The plan of the first experiment was, to make
the current of a little galvanic trough apparatus
[an early battery], commonly used in his lectures,
pass through a very thin platina [platinum] wire,
which was placed over a compass covered with
glass. The preparations for the experiment were
made, but some accident having hindered him
from trying it before the lecture, he intended to

---

[19]   *Ibid.*, p. 169.
[20]   *Ibid.*

defer it to another opportunity; yet during the lecture the probability of its success appeared stronger, so that he made the first experiment in the presence of the audience. The magnetical [magnetic] needle, though included in a box, was disturbed; but as the effect was very feeble, and must, before its law was discovered, seem very irregular, the experiment made no strong impression on the audience."[21]

Thus was electromagnetism, the connection between electricity and magnetism, discovered. One of the most important aspects of creative and critical thinking, however, is the influence of accepted experts in a given field. It is most difficult to "buck the tide" when the majority is in agreement with a particular theory being put forth by a strong personality, and yet that is precisely what creative and critical thinking often entails. How did the scientific community miss this basic relationship? Here is an explanation from one of the foremost French scientists of the day, André-Marie Ampére:

You are quite right [Ampére wrote to a friend] to say that it is inconceivable that for twenty years no one tried the action of the voltaic pile [source of electricity] on a magnet. I believe, however, that I can assign a cause for this; it lies in Coulomb's hypothesis on the nature of magnetic action; this hypothesis was believed as though it were a fact [and] it reflected [as in "rejected"] any idea of action between electricity and the

---

[21]   *Ibid.*, p. 139.

so-called magnetic wires. This prohibition was such that when M. Arago spoke of these new phenomena at the Institute, they were reflected… Every one decided that they were impossible.[22]

The question that was burning in the scientific community in both England and France concerned the mechanism for the relationship between electricity and magnetism. Theories abounded. Oersted had his theory of competing forces in constant tension, but the one theory that made the greatest impression on Faraday came from Ampére. His theory of two fluids captured many imaginations, including that of Faraday. But herein lies one of the most interesting aspects of Faraday's scientific abilities. Although he was a premier experimentalist, he was practically mathematically illiterate. He wrote to Ampére:

> With regard to your theory, it so soon becomes mathematical that it quickly gets beyond my reach.[23]

But Faraday was a master of logic and scientific induction—drawing explanations from a host of pieces of experimental information. He was asked to write an historical account of the new branch of science relating electricity and magnetism for the *Annals of Philosophy*. In order to do this, Faraday felt that he had to repeat all the critical experiments performed by Oersted, Arago, Ampére, and others to see how their theoretical explanations accorded with the

---

[22]   *Ibid.*, p. 142.
[23]   *Ibid.*, p. 143.

experimental results.[24] It was during this work that he started
to formulate his own understanding of the relationship between electricity and magnetism. After making a number of
novel experiments of his own, he eventually constructed the
final demonstration of electromagnetic induction—a toroid
(doughnut) of soft iron with a coil of copper wire on one side
(insulated from the iron) connected to a battery and a coil of
wire on the opposite side (insulated from the iron) connected
to a "galvanometer" to measure any flow of electricity in the
second coil. Indeed a change in the flow of electricity in the
first coil (by closing the circuit) created a changing magnetic
field in the iron core that induced a current in the second
coil that was measured by the galvanometer. The important
thing that Faraday noticed, that he and others had missed
before, was that is was the *change* in the fields that created
the desired effect. This was the stunning result that opened
up the opportunity for a massive variety of electromagnetic
industrial tools such as telegraphy, electric motors, radio, and
electricity generators.

This cursory look at Faraday's life offers but a hint of the
wealth of insight available in looking in detail at the intellectual development and thinking processes of a remarkable
contributor in the field of science. The following questions
help to focus on important parts of his life. In fact, they deal
with the ways the subject was influenced by mathematics,
science, psychology, economics, history, and literature. You
will notice three things about the questions chosen here: first,
that the information above may not be sufficient to answer
any of these questions adequately; second, that the same ap-
proximate set of questions is asked after each example; and
third, that many of the questions address the same general

---

[24]   See the section above entitled "I Don't Know, Let's Try It."

issue from different perspectives. This whole exercise is designed to point us toward the possibilities to be revealed in an integrated Human Drama Curriculum (HDC).

Before addressing a set of possible questions, however, it is absolutely critical to understand the subtle perspective that the HDC is trying to achieve. The student should be able to answer these questions easily from an in-depth study of the biographical subject and not as an end in themselves. The point is not to *answer the questions* but to *know the person.* One might say that if the student does not know the answers, he or she should reread the biography until the student becomes an "expert." It is not clear how a teacher might accomplish this, but the point is to keep the student from "looking up the answers." As students rarely reread anything, the value of repeated exposure to the subject's human drama only enhances the student's appreciation of that drama. How to encourage such in-depth study is an important aspect of the HDC. None of us "gets it" the first time. Unfortunately we usually try to cram in the basics, answer the questions, pass the test, even make an A, and move on. The point of the HDC is to offer the student the possibility of the joy of immersion and in-depth knowledge. To achieve this end the teacher might have the students develop and answer their own set of questions on aspects of the subject's life that particularly interested them. Developing strategies for getting the students to immerse in the life of the subject is an ongoing challenge of the HDC. As better strategies are developed, the curriculum becomes progressively more rewarding.

1. All accomplishment is achieved within the context of human physical limitations. What were Faraday's inherent physical characteristics and how did he deal with them? What are yours and how do or can you

deal with them?

2.   Personal power—such as wealth or position—is often a critical component of accomplishment. What was the nature and extent of Faraday's power and how did he use it? What is yours and how can you use it?

3.   Power struggles are often a component of accomplishment. What were the forces that opposed Faraday's progress and how did he overcome them? What are yours and how can you overcome them?

4.   Intellect is a critical element in accomplishment. What have we learned of Faraday's intellect, and how did it play a role in his accomplishments? What is your assessment of your intellect and how can you use it to its full potential?

5.   What was the role of "thirst for knowledge" in the life of Faraday? How did he satisfy it? How would you assess your own thirst? What might influence it?

6.   What was the role of environment in the life of Faraday and how did he utilize it to his advantage? How would you describe your own environment and how does it help or hinder you?

7.   The resources associated with the times (science, mathematics, technology, philosophy, arts, etc.) at Faraday's disposal were limitations to what he could accomplish. What were they and how did he make use of them. What resources do you have and how can you use them?

8.   Books have had an important influence on all achievers. What books were available to Faraday and how did he use them? What books are available to you and how do you plan to use them?

9.   Personal physical or psychological woundedness is

often a powerful theme in the lives of those of great achievement. How was this theme presented in the life of Faraday? How has your own woundedness influenced your own achievement?

10. Immersion and perseverance are critical aspects of any achievement. How did these factors express themselves in the life of Faraday? What opportunities have you taken or experienced in which your own achievement has been positively influenced by these factors? How can you plan to utilize them more fully?

11. What was the role of the subconscious in the creative thinking of Faraday? How does your subconscious help you and how can you foster its creative activity?

12. Often great personalities experience achievement in areas other than their primary livelihoods. Hobbies or other pastimes have resulted in considerable achievement. How did this aspect of achievement reflect itself in Faraday's life? How has it expressed itself in yours?

13. The juxtaposition of faith and rationality is always a challenge for students of Faraday to resolve. Thinking always requires some larger context in which to operate. How did religion and rationality inform Faraday's own thinking? How do you deal with these two aspects of life?

14. People usually have a strong influence—either positive or negative—on the direction of great achievers. What personalities influenced Faraday's growth and thinking processes? What people have influenced you and in what ways? How do you plan to place yourself in the sphere of "influential" people (not necessarily powerful people) who can help shape your life of achievement?

15. One often overlooked factor in human achievement is luck. How did luck play a part in the achievement of Faraday? How has it played a role in your life? How might you plan to put yourself in a position to maximize the presence of luck in your own life?

16. In the development of his electromagnetic theory, how did Faraday utilize analytical thinking to understand the pieces of the puzzle with which he was confronted?

17. Describe the pieces of the electromagnetic puzzle with which Faraday was confronted. Describe any other systems that have similar pieces.

18. How did Faraday utilize critical thinking in comparing the different theories (or proposed systems) of electricity and magnetism of his day to each other and to his own experimental evidence? How do these similar systems relate to each other?

19. How did he utilize creative thinking to make the leap from existing theories to a new understanding that opened the door to future scientific and technological achievements? How might Faraday have filled in the missing pieces of his electromagnetic puzzle with pieces from other similar systems?

Human Drama in Mathematics - René Descartes

In most cases in mathematics we only know about the details of the lives of mathematicians who lived after the 16th Century. While the lives of Archimedes and Euclid would certainly shed important light on their achievements, the information is not present. One of the earliest mathematicians about whom we have considerable biographical information is René Descartes, who offers an unusual example of a man of diverse interests, as well as a remarkable analytical, critical, and creative mind. While his philosophical contributions are certainly on a par with his mathematical contribution to analytical geometry, it is the latter that will be of central interest here.

Descartes was born in 1596 near Tours, France, to an old, respectable, but not wealthy, family. His mother died shortly after his birth, and he spent his childhood under the tutelage of his father and nurse. He was a fragile child who needed more sleep than his peers. When eight years old, he was sent to a Jesuit school where the unusually supportive relationship with the rector allowed him to spend his mornings in bed thinking until ready to join his classmates. He not only became proficient in the classics, but also began his intellectual journey of skepticism toward the humanities as they were then taught. His concern was more for solving problems than displaying a plethora of facts.[25] The following quotation captures his state:

> I entirely abandoned the study of letters. Resolving to seek no knowledge other than that of which could be found in myself or else in the great book of the world, I spent the rest of my youth traveling, visiting courts and armies, mixing with people of diverse temperaments and ranks, gathering various experiences, testing myself in the situations which fortune offered me, and at all times reflecting upon whatever came

---

[25]   This shift in emphasis in the life of Descartes is remarkably similar to the shift in emphasis being proposed in the HDC.

my way so as to derive some profit from it.[26]

It was this drive that eventually led him to his own brand
of empirical philosophy and mathematics. His basic philosophical question became, "How do we *know* anything?"
And even more important, "How can we *learn* anything?"[27]
Out of this rational skepticism Descartes arrived at the conclusion that the only things that can be learned are those that
result from rigorous experimentation and mathematical expression. Having sufficient financial resources, he left school
at 17 and by 18 had determined to discover his own truths by
experience.

After a period of frivolous living followed by intense
mathematical investigation, he found solace in the military.
Somehow in various military settings he was allowed a kind
of mental tranquility. One can only surmise that the juxtaposition of the order and relative simplicity of military life
with the opportunity to ponder deeper connections offered
a fertile environment for Descartes. Understanding why this
might be true for one of his intellect and background is certainly one of the considerable challenges in interpreting his
life. His relationship with Isaac Beeckman stands out as important in Descartes' process of formation, as indicated by
the following quotation from Vrooman's biography:

> ...Beeckman proved to be the catalyst neces-
> sary to reawaken Descartes' enthusiasm and en-
> courage him to undertake new enterprises. Sev-
> eral months later he [Descartes] expressed his

---

[26]   René Descartes, "Discourse on the Method," *The Philosophical
Works of Descartes* (Cambridge University Press, 1911), p. 86.
[27]   E.T. Bell, *Men of Mathematics* (Simon and Shuster, 1937), p. 37.

gratitude thus: "To speak truthfully, you alone have drawn me from my idleness and made me remember what I had learned and almost forgotten; when my mind was wandering from serious occupations, you brought it back to the right path. If I produce anything of merit, you will be entitled to claim it entirely for yourself."[28]

We do know that during this time he experienced a profound "conversion" as the result of three dreams. Bell expresses the importance of this event as follows:

The story of Descartes' "conversion"—if it may be called that—is extremely curious. On St. Martin's Eve, November 10, 1619, Descartes experienced three vivid dreams which, he says, changed the whole current of his life.... No doubt the Freudians have analyzed these dreams, but it seems unlikely that any analysis in the classical Viennese manner could throw further light on the invention of analytic geometry, in which we are chiefly interested here.[29]

Out of it all Descartes says he was filled with "enthusiasm" (probably intended in a mystic sense) and that there had been revealed to him ... the magic key which would unlock the treasure house of nature and put him in possession of the true foundation, at least, of all the sciences. What was the marvelous key? Descartes himself does

---

[28]   Jack R Vrooman, *René Descartes: A Biography* (G. P. Putnam's Sons, 1970), p. 49.
[29]   Bell, p. 39.

not seem to have told anyone explicitly, but it is
usually believed to have been nothing less than
the application of algebra to geometry, analytic
geometry in short and, more generally, the exploration of natural phenomena by mathematics,
of which mathematical physics today is the most
highly developed example.[30]

November 10, 1619, then is the official birthday of analytic
geometry, and therefore also of modern mathematics. Eigh-
teen years were to pass before the method was published.

The fact that Descartes' writings were placed on the Index
of Prohibited Books by Pope Alexander VII in 1663 (13 years
after Descartes' death) has indicated to many observers that
he was estranged from the Catholic Church and possibly an
atheist.

Nothing could be further from the truth. His religious beliefs were unaffectedly simple in spite of
his rational skepticism. He compared his religion,
indeed, to the nurse from whom he had received
it, and declared that he found it as comforting to
lean upon one as on the other.[31]

It was, however, in 1633 that Galileo was forced to re-
cant his support for the Copernican understanding of the
solar system. Descartes was mystified that the Pope would
be opposed to an understanding that was so patently evident
to Descartes. He delayed publication of his masterwork, *Le
Monde*, in deference to his own belief in the infallibility of

30   *Ibid.*, p. 40.
31   *Ibid.*, p. 42.

the Pope. Finally in 1637 at the encouragement of his friends, he published the work under the title (translated), *A Discourse on the Method of rightly conducting the Reason and seeking Truth in the Sciences.*

Given Descartes' constant flirtation with death on the battlefield, one should not neglect the influence of luck on the fact of his publishing his works at all. Certainly history is replete with examples of lost or unfulfilled achievement. Here is a case in which one stray bullet or cannon ball could have deprived the world of the thoughts of a great genius.

The following set of questions asked about the life of Faraday can also be asked of Descartes:

1. All accomplishment is achieved within the context of human physical limitations. What were Descartes' inherent physical limitations and how did he deal with them?

2. Personal power, such as wealth or position, is often a critical component of accomplishment. What was the nature and extent of Descartes' power and how did he use it?

3. Power struggles are often a component of accomplishment. What were the forces that opposed Descartes' progress and how did he overcome them?

4. Intellect is a critical element in accomplishment. What have you learned of Descartes' intellect, and how did it play a role in his accomplishments?

5. What was the role of "thirst for knowledge" in the life of Descartes? How was it satisfied?

6. What was the role of environment in the life of Descartes and how did he utilize it to his advantage?

7. The times and the resources (science, mathematics, technology, philosophy, arts, etc.) at Descartes'

disposal were limitations to what he could accomplish. What were they and how did he make use of them.

8. Books have had an important influence on all achievers. What books were available to Descartes and how did he use them?

9. Personal physical and psychological woundedness is often a powerful theme in the lives of those of great achievement. How has this theme been present in the life of Descartes?

10. Immersion and perseverance have been critical aspects of any achievement. How have these factors expressed themselves in the life of Descartes?

11. What was the role of the subconscious in the creative thinking of Descartes?

12. Often great personalities experience achievement in areas other than their primary livelihoods. Hobbies or other pastimes have resulted in considerable achievement. How did this aspect of achievement reflect itself in Descartes' life?

13. The juxtaposition of faith and rationality is always a challenge for students of Descartes to resolve. Thinking always requires some larger context in which to operate. How did religion and rationality inform Descartes' own thinking and why was his rational approach perceived as a threat to the Church?

14. People usually have a strong influence (either positive or negative) on the direction of great achievers. What personalities influenced Descartes' growth and thinking processes?

15. One often overlooked factor in human achievement is luck. How did luck play a part in the achievement of Descartes?

16. In the development of his analytical geometry, how did Descartes utilize analytical thinking in understanding the geometric methodologies of his day?

17. Describe the pieces of the geometric/mathematical puzzle with which Descartes was confronted. Describe any other systems that have similar pieces.

18. How did Descartes utilize critical thinking in comparing these methodologies in order to see needs and opportunities? How do these similar systems relate to each other?

19. How did Descartes utilize creative thinking in developing his new analytical geometry? How might Descartes have filled in the missing pieces of his analytical geometry puzzle with pieces from other similar systems?

Human Drama in Literature - William Faulkner[32]

While we might find the lives of great authors of interest, we rarely see them as an essential part of the study of their output. To see these lives as the driving force of the entire creative endeavor is an essential part of the HDC. The relationship of the life and writings of William Falkner offers a particularly fruitful opportunity within the HDC. One can apply analytical, critical, and creative thinking processes to assessing Faulkner's genius by delving into three historical contexts: first, the historical era during which Faulkner lived and wrote his novels; second, the autobiographical details of the writer's life; and lastly, the historical periods the writer expresses in his works.

---

[32] Bob Muldoon kindly contributed most of this essay on Faulkner.

William Faulkner lived from 1897 until 1962. He was born, raised, and lived the bulk of his life in Oxford, Mississippi, only leaving it sporadically for brief periods—the Royal Air Force in 1918, Hollywood forays as a screenplay writer in order to earn money, and a brief stint as "Writer in Residence" at the University of Virginia late in his life. The rest of the time Faulkner immersed himself in the murky waters of the Deep South. The decline and gradual rehabilitation of the South formed the interconnected cultural pattern that became the backdrop of his understanding of the human drama. While his social culture remained circumscribed, his life spanned many historical benchmarks: World War I, the Roaring Twenties, the Great Depression, World War II, the Cold War, and the Nuclear Age. He experienced the advent of the automobile, airplane, the space age, radio, talking pictures, television, and the early stages of computers; and weapons of mass destruction that potentially place our entire civilization in jeopardy. All of these historical benchmarks influenced his work.[33]

So how did Faulkner stumble upon his epic achievement? Faulkner never received a high school diploma, although he did attend some classes at the University of Mississippi in Oxford after his service with the Royal Air Force. "Faulkner taught himself, largely, as he says, by 'undirected and uncorrelated reading'."[34] These resources included Keats, Balzac, Flaubert, Swinburne, Verlaine, Mallarmé, Wilde, Housman, Joyce, Eliot, Sherwood Anderson, E. E. Cummings—and later, Hemingway, Dos Passos, and F. Scott Fitzgerald.[35] He

---

[33]   Malcolm Cowley, *The Portable Faulkner* (The Viking Press, 1946), p. vii.
[34]   *Ibid.*, p. ix..
[35]   *Ibid.*, p. x.

"was not so much composing stories for the public as telling them to himself—like a lonely child in his imaginary world, but also like a writer of genius."[36]

Faulkner's family life also had a strong impact on his development:

> For Billy [Faulkner], books and stories opened up a rainbow world of boundless imaginings. In the cavernous library of his grandfather's place, he nourished his imagination on volumes of Scott and Dumas.[37]

> [Faulkner's] mother became the boy's devoted teacher, asking his devotion in return...She taught him to read, guiding him confidently through the early primers and Grimms' fairy tales, then introducing him to the magic world of Charles Dickens—all before he started school, at the age of eight.[38]

The setting for the novels that comprise his epic saga was Faulkner's mythical kingdom—Yoknapatawpha County, Mississippi, circa 1820 to 1950—a parable or legend of all the Deep South. The historical era he depicted covered "symbols of the Old South, of war and reconstruction, of commerce and machinery destroying the standards of the past."[39] The Faulkner canon embodied the Southern Agrarians' major

---

[36]   *Ibid.*, p. xi.

[37]   Stephen B. Oates, *William Faulkner: The Man and the Artist* (Harper & Row, 1987), p. 7.

[38]   *Ibid.*, pp. 6-7.

[39]   *Ibid.*, p. viii.

premise—rural versus industrialized society. The citizens of his mythical society are storekeepers, mechanics, professional men, farmers, and woodmen. Their main commercial products are baled cotton and lumber. The people live in grand plantation houses (only a few), relics of another age, wooden farmhouses (some) and poorly housed tenant dwellings (many), similar to the slave quarters of the not-so-distant past. Seventeen of Faulkner's 25 novels are wholly concerned with the County and its people, as are dozens of his uncollected short stories spanning the years 1929 to 1962. Balzac's *Comédie Humaine's* "Scenes of Parisian Life," "Scenes of Provincial Life," and "Scenes of Private Life" may have inspired Faulkner's series of novels and short stories.

Faulkner's universe can be depicted by the following table:

Social Hierarchy	Fictional Families
Planters and their descendants	Compson-Sartoris saga
Townspeople of Jefferson City	McCaslin saga
Poor whites	Snopes saga
Indians	Ratliff-Bundren saga
Negroes	Black descendants of Caruthers McCaslin

All of these families and their fractured status in the tumultuous social hierarchy of the Deep South resonated in a discordant melody hummed throughout in Faulkner's operatic masterworks. In the contrast between the antebellum period, reconstruction, and the first half of the twentieth century, Faulkner's "characters carry, whether heroes or villains, a curious sense of submission to their fate."[40]

"Each novel, each long or short story, seems to reveal more than it states explicitly, and to have a subject bigger than itself."[41] "All the separate works are like blocks of marble from the same quarry: they show the veins and faults of the mother rock."[42] According to André Gide in *The New American Novelists*, "There is not one of Faulkner's characters who properly speaking has a soul."[43]—that is, not one of them exercises the faculty of conscious choice between good and evil. And yet Faulkner has great empathy for his characters because he has a "brooding love for the land where he was born and reared and where, unlike other writers of his generation, he has chosen to spend his life."[44] Accordingly, his novels have the quality of being lived, absorbed, and remembered—rather than merely observed.

Faulkner summed up his vision in his memorable Nobel Prize address in 1950. He espoused an obstinate faith that "man will not only endure: he will prevail."[45] "What Faulkner regarded as his ultimate subject is not the South or its destiny, however much they occupied his mind, but rather the human situations as revealed in Southern terms."[46] So here is the essence of William Faulkner's life, times, and works as eloquently stated in his own words:

> Today's writer must write about the old verities and truths of the heart, the old universal truths lacking which any story is ephemeral and

---

[40]   *Ibid.*, p. xxiii.
[41]   *Ibid.*, p. xv.
[42]   *Ibid.*, p. xxiii.
[43]   *Ibid.*, p. xxv.
[44]   *Ibid.*, p. xxxi.
[45]   *Ibid.*, p. xxxii.
[46]   *Ibid.*, p. xxxii.

doomed—love and honor and pity and pride and
compassion and sacrifice.[47]

> The primary job that any writer faces is to tell
> you a story out of human experience—I mean by
> that, universal mutual experience, the anguish-
> es and troubles and griefs of the human heart,
> which is universal, without regard to race or time
> or condition. He wants to tell you something
> which has seemed to him so true, so moving, ei-
> ther comic or tragic, that it's worth preserving.[48]

Finally, Ralph Ellison's comment on the Oates biography
of Faulkner captures the essence of the HDC.

> I found Stephen B. Oates's *William Falkner: The
> Man and the Artist* engrossing reading from be-
> ginning to end. Both because it conveys insights
> into the complex processes of literary technique
> and artistic imagination through which a great
> American writer made stories and novels out of
> the emotion and insights gleaned from his living,
> and because Stephen Oates's biographical skills
> swept me along with something of the narrative
> thrust and psychological illumination that are
> characteristic of Faulkner's fiction.[49]

*It is from precisely these kinds of biographical resources that the
HDC will be built.* The same set of questions can then be applied to Falkner.

---

[47]   *Ibid.*, p. xxxi.
[48]   Oates, p. vii.
[49]   *Ibid.*, dust jacket.

1. All accomplishment is achieved within the context of human physical limitations. What were Faulkner's inherent physical limitations and how did he deal with them?

2. Personal power, such as wealth or position, is often a critical component of accomplishment. What was the nature and extent of Faulkner's power and how did he use it?

3. Power struggles are often a component of accomplishment. What were the forces that opposed Faulkner's progress and how did he overcome them?

4. Intellect is a critical element in accomplishment. What have you learned of Faulkner's intellect, and how did it play a role in his accomplishments?

5. What was the role of "thirst for knowledge" in the life of Faulkner? How was it satisfied?

6. What was the role of environment in the life of Faulkner and how did he utilize it to his advantage?

7. The times and the resources (science, mathematics, technology, philosophy, arts, etc.) at Faulkner's disposal were limitations to what he could accomplish. What were they and how did he make use of them?

8. Books have had an important influence on all achievers. What books were available to Faulkner and how did he use them?

9. Personal physical and psychological woundedness is often a powerful theme in the lives of those of great achievement. How has this theme been present in the life of Faulkner?

10. Immersion and perseverance have been critical aspects of any achievement. How have these factors expressed themselves in the life of Faulkner?

11. What was the role of the subconscious in the creative thinking of Faulkner?

12. Often great personalities experience achievement in areas other than their primary livelihoods. Hobbies or other pastimes have resulted in considerable achievement. How did this aspect of achievement reflect itself in Faulkner's life?

13. The juxtaposition of faith and rationality is always a challenge for students of Faulkner to resolve. Thinking always requires some larger context in which to operate. How did religion and rationality inform Faulkner's own thinking?

14. People usually have a strong influence (either positive or negative) on the direction of great achievers. What personalities influenced Faulkner's growth and thinking processes?

15. One often overlooked factor in human achievement is luck. How did luck play a part in the achievement of Faulkner?

16. In the development of his series of novels located in the fictional Yoknapatawpha County, Mississippi, how did Faulkner utilize analytical thinking in understanding his characters?

17. Describe a character in one of his novels. Where would he have found similar characters as models for his fictional ones?

18. How did he utilize critical thinking in comparing his fictional characters among themselves and to people he knew? How might the fictional characters have compared to the real ones?

19. How did he utilize creative thinking in stepping outside the culture and personalities of his native

environment to tell universal truths that have broad value and appeal? How might he have made changes in the characteristics of the real characters to make his fictional characters capture a more vivid rendering of the deeper truths he was trying to portray?

Human Drama in History - Peter the Great[50]

Historical leaders are perennial objects of our interest. The results of their lives as politicians, statesmen, monarchs, revolutionaries, dictators and/or conquerors are laid out for all to see. History books tell of their achievements or failures, but we are always left with the gnawing questions regarding not so much when or what but why or how. Peter the Great of Russia was a man whose accomplishments are exposed for the world to see, but the personal driving forces behind those accomplishments remain historically and eternally mysterious. He was a force of nature, possessing phenomenal energy and complexity. In Robert K. Massie's epic biography[51], the author's final statement on his subject's essence is a question, "How does one judge the endless roll of the ocean or the mighty power of the whirlwind?"[52] Alexander Pushkin assesses Peter's essence thus: "Eternal toiler upon the throne of Russia."[53] Peter himself makes the following self-assessment to a foreign ambassador who unctuously flatters the emperor; "Flattery says much of every king when he is present. My object is not to see the fair side of things, but to know what judgment is formed of me on the opposite side of the

---

[50]   Bob Muldoon kindly contributed most of this essay on Peter the Great.

[51]   Robert K. Massie, *Peter the Great* (Alfred A. Knopf, 1980), p. xi.

[52]   *Ibid.*, p. 855.

[53]   *Ibid.*, p. xii.

question."[54] He also comments on his mission in life in a letter to his confidant, Prince Menshikov, "It is an age of gold in which we are living—without the loss of a single instant, we devote all our energies to work."[55]

Peter was born in Moscow in 1672, the second son of Tsar Alexis, into a traditional Russian culture steeped in ancient traditions and social hierarchy. While still a vast region, Russia of the day was considered by those outside observers as backward and out of touch with what was then considered to be the "modern world." Peter was raised in the privileged ruling class with access to virtually unlimited resources. Although never of robust health and said to have been afflicted by something resembling epilepsy, his desire and stamina as a child were a reflection of his great energy as an adult. He was educated by a number to tutors, some of whom introduced him to a wide range of western ideas. At the family's summer estate Peter indulged in elaborate war games with friends and other "conscripts." As he matured so did his personal regiment until it became an important part of the Russian military establishment. As can be seen below, he took his place within the regiment in a wholly unorthodox manner:

> Peter plunged enthusiastically into this activity, wanting to participate fully at every level. Rather than taking for himself the rank of colonel, he enlisted in the Preobrazhensky Regiment [that he had formed] at the lowest grade, as a drummer boy, where he could play with gusto the instrument he loved. Eventually, he promoted himself to artilleryman or bombardier, so that he could

---

54   *Ibid.*, p. 855.
55   *Ibid.*

fire the weapon which made the most noise and did the most damage. In barracks or field, he allowed no distinction between himself and others. He performed the same duties, stood his turn at watch day and night, slept in the same tent and ate the same food. When earthworks were built, Peter dug with a shovel. When the regiment went on parade, Peter stood in the ranks, taller than the others but otherwise undistinguished.[56]

As he matured he became an extraordinarily tall and vigorous man—6'7" tall with a strong, erect body—but he suffered from severe seizures his entire life. His complex nature is captured by Massie's statement of opposites, "impetuous and stubborn, bawdy and stern, relentless in his perseverance, constantly on the move, inspecting, organizing, encouraging, criticizing, commanding, capable of the greatest generosity and the greatest cruelty."[57] Peter abhorred the trappings of majesty—he was most content working at his forge or at shipyards hewing timbers in concert with common laborers. When he ventured forth to explore the cities and courts of Europe, he traveled incognito, desperately attempting to avoid the fanfare that an emperor must endure. When commanding armies in the field or engaging in naval warfare on the seas, he never assumed the highest rank as commander in chief, preferring to be in a subservient position. In his personal life, Peter took Catherine, a robust and gentle peasant, as his mistress; then, later, he married her, elevated her to empress, and then saw that she succeeded him as empress of all Russia upon his death. His relationship with his eldest

---

[56]   *Ibid.*, p. 69.

[57]   *Ibid.*, dust cover.

son Alexis, heir to the throne was tormented and, ultimately resulted in the son's death for treason.

Out of this complex giant emerges the drama of an extraordinary human being. His accomplishments were numerous. As a visionary statesman, Peter changed Russian society, government, and the economy. Leaders were selected through merit and accomplishment, rather than through noble birth. Westerners from all of Europe were recruited to build a new, modern Russia. Peter himself printed the first Russian newspaper, created factories, established schools and universities, hospitals, museums, and libraries. He even edited and published books. As a maker of the modern world, and imbued with Western ideas, Peter created the first Russian Navy and opened up the Baltic and Black Seas to Russian merchant ships. As a great military commander, Peter ultimately won a 20-year war with his archenemy, Charles XII of Sweden, and he stopped the encroachment of the Ottoman Empire by defeating the Sublime Porte of the Turkish Sultan (Constantinople). Also on the world stage, Peter gained the respect, and sometimes the enmity, of all the great European rulers of his age, especially Louis XIV of France and William III and George I of England. Finally, out of a swamp, Peter created the glorious European-inspired capital of St. Petersburg. This westernmost Russian city defined Russia as a formidable world power by the time of Peter's death in 1725. In the 43-year span of his reign—from a ten-year-old co-tsar to the Emperor of all Russia—Peter transposed his expanded nation from a backwater, medieval hodgepodge of unconnected territories to one of the premier world powers. His relentless curiosity and phenomenal energy changed the world.

The major historical events spanned by his life include the

reign of Louis XIV of France and the development of central government, as well as the development of the New World. Intellectually he experienced in some way the expansion of knowledge in the Enlightenment, including major advances in mathematics and science by Fermat, Pascal, Newton, and Leibniz. His use of available resources is indicated by the following quotation:

> The Tsar himself has collected books all his life, and especially on his visits to Germany, France, Holland and other countries in the West. His personal library included works on a wide range of subjects, including military and naval affairs, science, history, medicine, law and religion... Ancient monasteries of Russia [contributed] old manuscripts, chronicles and books...After his death, his library became the nucleus of the Russian Academy of Science [library]."[58]

Perhaps a final assessment of Peter's essence is best stated by Peter himself:

> I am represented as a cruel tyrant; this is the opinion foreign nations have formed of me. But how can they judge? They do not know the circumstances I was in at the beginning of my reign, how many people opposed my designs, counteracted my most useful projects and obliged me to be severe. But I never treated anyone cruelly or gave proofs of tyranny. On the contrary, I have always asked the assistance of such of my subjects

---

[58] *Ibid.*, p. 837.

as have shown marks of intelligence and patri-
otism, and who, doing justice to the rectitude
of my intentions, have been disposed to second
them. Nor have I ever failed to testify my gratitude by loading them with favor.[59]

There have been few who engaged their time as energeti-
cally as Peter, so the central question for the Human Drama
Curriculum is, "What do we take away from a detailed study
of one person's life?" As Peter himself implies above, having
a clear understanding of the "circumstances" in which he
functioned is essential to understanding the true nature of his
accomplishments. Consider again the same set of questions
that were applied to Faraday, Descartes, and Faulkner that
are clearly an attempt to get at the circumstances in which
each had to function. In addition, from an historical stand-
point, we might see that a vast "sea change" or paradigm shift
took place in Russia under Peter's rule. Such a deep-seated
change that a society can never reverse is nothing short of
the kinds of revolutionary paradigm shifts that we have seen
in the scientific revolutions instigated by Copernicus and
Einstein. In fact the idea of the importance of such a shift
(as articulated by Thomas Kuhn[60]) could form the basis of a
new question (#22). While it is not necessary that the lives
of individuals involve such paradigm shifts, it is clear that we
should be looking for them when they occur. If we were to
consider this same question with regard to Faraday, Descartes,
and Faulkner, we might find the exercise extremely fruitful.
This process of recognizing a universal principle and adding

---

[59]   *Ibid.*, p. 855.
[60]   Thomas S. Kuhn, "The Structure of Scientific Revolutions,"
Foundations of the Unity of Science, vol. 2, (University of Chicago Press Chicago, 1970), pp. 52 – 272.

a question to reflect this new understanding is just one way in which the HDC becomes a living and evolving process, rather than a static cookie-cutter approach.

1. All accomplishment is achieved within the context of human physical limitations. What were Peter's inherent physical characteristics and how did they help or hinder him?

2. Personal power, such as wealth or position, is often a critical component of accomplishment. What was the nature and extent of Peter's power and how did he use it?

3. Power struggles are often a component of accomplishment. What were the forces that opposed Peter's progress and how did he overcome them?

4. Intellect is a critical element in accomplishment. What have you learned of Peter's intellect, and how did it play a role in his accomplishments?

5. What was the role of "thirst for knowledge" in the life of Peter the Great? How was it satisfied?

6. What was the role of environment in the life of Peter and how did he utilize it to his advantage?

7. The times and the resources (science, mathematics, technology, philosophy, arts, etc.) at Peter's disposal were limitations to what he could accomplish. What were they and how did he make use of them.

8. Books have had an important influence on all achievers. What books were available to Peter and how did he use them?

9. Personal physical and psychological woundedness is often a powerful theme in the lives of those of great achievement. How has this theme been present in the life of Peter?

10. Immersion and perseverance have been critical aspects

of any achievement. How have these factors expressed themselves in the life of Peter?

11. What was the role of the subconscious in the creative thinking of Peter the Great?

12. Often great personalities experience achievement in areas other than their primary livelihoods. Hobbies or other pastimes have resulted in considerable achievement. How did this aspect of achievement reflect itself in Peter's life?

13. The juxtaposition of faith and rationality is always a challenge for students of Peter the Great to resolve. Thinking always requires some larger context in which to operate. How did religion and rationality inform Peter's own thinking?

14. People usually have a strong influence (either positive or negative) on the direction of great achievers. What personalities influenced Peter's growth and thinking processes?

15. One often overlooked factor in human achievement is luck. How did luck play a part in the achievement of Peter?

16. In the development of his policies for Russia that were radical departure from the culture in which he grew up, how did Peter utilize analytical thinking to understand Russia's existing challenges and the need for change?

17. Describe the characteristics of one aspect of traditional Russian life (system) with which Peter was confronted. Describe any other European system that had similar characteristics.

18. How did he utilize critical thinking in comparing the Russia of his day to the European culture of his day

to recognize needs and opportunities for his country?

19. How do these two similar systems relate to each other?

20. How did he utilize creative thinking in understanding how to move his native land in a direction that recognized the existing Russian culture and its inherent resistance as well as the unique applications of European culture that would fit with his country's past?

21. How might Peter have filled in the missing pieces of his own system with pieces from other similar systems?

22. How could the accomplishments of Peter be seen as a paradigm shift, either local (in Russia) or global (for the whole world)?

Human Drama - Conclusions

There are several critical points that must be stressed if this approach is to be a meaningful enhancement of the educational process:

1. The availability of sufficiently detailed biographical information is central. All too often biographers do not press the limited information to form some kind of conclusion concerning the subject's thinking processes. Often, as will be seen in the next section, biographical materials will have to be conditioned for the grade level in which they are being used.

2. The introduction of HDAC to any curriculum is a process that will start slowly and gradually build materials and influence. The development of meaningful curricular units may require considerable work, but once they are developed they become a central part of the overall curriculum and of growing importance. Units therefore would be continually added to the overall curriculum. Thus the addition of new units would always be a net addition to the educational experience of the school as a whole.

3. Once the three styles of analytical, critical and creative thinking are articulated or at least surmised in the lives of those persons being studied, the most important part of the HDC is to allow the students to

describe these processes and the systems on which they operated in order to draw conclusions about ways in which they might apply the same kinds of cognitive and systems approaches to other situations.

4. The whole object is for the student to develop a portfolio of systems concepts and ways to think about them analytically, critically and creatively. This *reference library of the mind* is the fundamental set of thinking resources that allows the students to approach and solve problems deliberately in a host of new situations. It is this aspect of the HDC that gives it its power. As one product of the HDC, the students could begin to organize knowledge around general systems structures and gradually add to a written description of these structures.[61, 62]

5. The HDC lends itself particularly to the introduction of the dramatic arts into every aspect of the curriculum. Students could be assigned the task of taking one aspect of the subject's life and character and creating a small "drama" to reflect that aspect. For example, Descartes' propensity to stay in bed to meditate could turn into a lively and humorous five-minute skit in which others try to wrench him out of bed in the morning. Faraday's tendency to experiment could turn into a skit about his experimenting with

---

[61]   I have suggested the possibility of developing a *General Systems Encyclopedia* that would be a repository of such systems. Jonathan S. Fletcher, 1985, An encyclopedia of general systems. Bulletin of the Society for General Systems Research, v. 16, no. 1, pp. 8. Note that the current name of the organization is the International Society for the Systems Sciences.

[62]   Jonathan S. Fletcher, 1986, Developing a general systems encyclopedia as a tool for an integrated liberal arts curriculum. Proceedings of 1986 Annual Meeting, Society for General Systems Research, v. 2, pp M44-M46.

everything in sight. As an expression of the student's license to use humor and caricature, these exercises could be great fun and leave a lasting impression of the unique characteristics of the subject. I still remember a skit I was involved with in my high school French class in which a duel was initiated by the statement, "Choisissez votre défense!" (Choose your weapon!) These kinds of skits would certainly become more sophisticated as the students grow in maturity. Several dimensions of the little mini-dramas could be introduced, for example: show or make up a problem that the subject had to overcome (e.g. George Washington's boat got stuck in the mud when he was trying to cross the Delaware) or show how a change of luck could have reversed the entire outcome (e.g. Some drunk Hessian just happened to stumble onto an overlook and saw the advancing Americans).

6. The list of possible biographies that could be studied is indeed endless. The fundamental process in developing the HDC would be for those involved in the program to do research into the possibilities, decide on the ones that seem most fruitful, assemble the biographical materials, and develop the best ways to present the unit. Throughout this ongoing development process the students should be involved in researching, choosing and organizing these materials. The following is just a taste of possible biographies that could be considered:[63]

   • Abraham Lincoln
   • Indira Gandhi

---

[63]   I recognize the need to balance cultural, race, and gender considerations, but we are always somewhat constrained by history itself. With some creativity, even this limitation can be overcome.

- Andrew Jackson
- Douglas McArthur
- Golda Meir
- Oliver Wendell Holmes
- Benjamin Franklin
- Frederick Douglas
- Guatama Buddha
- Marie Curie
- Winston Churchill
- Adolf Hitler[64]
- Joseph Stalin
- Harriet Tubman
- Mother Teresa
- Lucrezia Borgia
- Luciano Pavarotti
- Helen Keller
- Martin Luther
- Ludwig von Beethoven
- Vincent Van Gogh
- Emily Dickenson
- Booker T. Washington
- Muhammad
- Jesus of Nazareth[65]
- Albert Einstein
- Mohandas Gandhi
- Napoleon Bonaparte

---

[64]   All the biographies are not necessarily of nice guys or gals. The power of understanding the origins of evil and destruction are just as important as understanding the origins of goodness and creativity.

[65]   From a strictly biographical point of view, this is a story of epic proportions that can be discussed from a human perspective, independent of the faith issues that surround his life and death. The same would be true for other religious leaders.

- Billy Graham
- Mao Zedong
- Chiang Kai-shek
- Martin Luther King, Jr.
- Catherine the Great
- Blaise Pascal
- Isaac Newton
- Queen Elizabeth I
- Theodore Roosevelt
- Joan of Arc
- Abraham Lincoln
- Pope John Paul II
- Franklin Delano Roosevelt
- Eleanor Roosevelt
- Nelson Mandela
- Queen Victoria
- George Washington
- Maria Callas
- Leonardo da Vinci
- Eva Peron
- Socrates
- Alexander the Great
- Cleopatra
- Christopher Columbus
- Queen Isabella of Spain
- Michelangelo
- Louisa May Alcott
- Andrew Carnegie
- Beatrix Potter
- Cecil Rhodes
- And, last but not least—Barney Barnato[66]

---

[66]   You might have to look that one up, but he in some way is

7. There are two critical criteria for choosing biographical materials:

    *   The life of the person must be sufficiently interesting and broad in scope to offer meaningful insights to the students.
    *   There must exist sufficient critical biographical materials so that one might "get at" the inner workings of the thinking processes taking place in that individual.

8. The most basic assertion of the HDC is that one learns more by immersion and concentration than by survey. It is better from a pedagogical point of view to learn a few things well than many things superficially. The boldness of the HDC approach is that in order to spend time on one personality one would have to sacrifice some areas of the traditional curriculum. To be blunt, we feel that it would be much better for a student never to have heard of Keats and to have studied Frost in detail than to have dabbled in both. The student with tremendous thinking skills can always go fill in the holes, but cannot go back and create *ex nihilo* the fundamental thinking skills. Most of us have had to spend many years drawing high-level conclusions about the thinking process after a traditional education "exposed" us to much—but immersed us in little.

9. One interesting aspect of the normal educational approach—using textbooks that present the results of the human drama and not the drama itself—is that we

---

related to the Rhoades Scholarship, the DeBeers diamond organization, and the early history of South Africa and represents a fascinating story of achievement and tragedy.

usually never keep the textbooks. One of the objectives of the HDC is that at least in the upper grades, the students should, after they graduate, have a library of biographies that they can keep, return to, and add to throughout their lives. Personal libraries are one sign of an educated individual who views his or her education as a lifelong process. A related objective is that each student will develop a certain affinity with various personalities to which he or she is being exposed and will want to collect additional materials relating to that person, thus deriving deeper stimulation and encouragement from further details of the life of another.

10. The HDC is based on the premise that we are instinctively driven to read the works of an author—whether literary, historical, scientific, or mathematical—once we know the compelling drama of his or her life. How can one not thirst to read the *Discourse* of Descartes once one knows the drama out of which it flowed? How can one not be driven to read the novels of Faulkner after having delved into his own personal drama out of which these novels flowed?

11. The HDC is not about others as much as it is about the student. We learn how others fulfilled their potential so that we might learn about who we are and how we can fulfill our own potential. Facts and figures are of secondary importance. With the Internet that factual information is readily available with a few keystrokes. Struggle, effort, persistence, and *thinking* are of primary importance. The point here is that students, by learning well the details of a few lives, have benchmarks to start to compare and contrast (critical

thinking) the lives of others with their own lives.

12. The HDC is essentially about figuring things out—seeing how others figured things out and then applying those lessons to figuring things out for oneself. The mantra discussed above, "I don't know, let's try it!" is compelling and a central theme of the HDC. It is about *thinking*—pulling things apart to see how they tick, comparing and contrasting the parts of the puzzle, thinking about various ways of putting the pieces together in a new way to solve a problem, figuring out the most fruitful approach, trying it, assessing the results, adjusting the plan and trying it again. This is how people have solved problems throughout history. This is how people solve problems today. And this is how students should be taught to solve their own problems and challenges. This is the point of the HDC.

13. To accomplish this thinking aspect of learning, the HDC stresses systems thinking. One aspect of this approach is reflected in the fact that the same set of questions is asked for each biographical subject. The implication is that the set of questions represents some sort of *universe of possibilities*, and it is important to consider each one, whether or not there is a specific answer articulated in the biographical materials. Systems tools help the student *know where to look* intellectually for factors that might inform the solution to any problem. By dealing in universes, the student always knows to seek and explore such universes in addressing issues. As the set of questions is applied to different cases, it is anticipated that it will be refined and expanded.

14. Both biographies and biographers become valid

subjects of study. Biographers must create a literary work out of fragments of information. In doing so they must fill in the blanks and interpret the whole, thus reconstructing the human drama—not unlike the work of an archeologist. There is, therefore, plenty of room for spinning the story in one direction or another, depending on the purpose, background, or inclination of the biographer. The HDC should, at least in the upper grades, start to examine this additional dimension of the materials being studied. We never seem to do this with textbooks. The teacher does this work while choosing a "good" textbook that reflects the "bias" of the individual teacher, school, or local culture. The student becomes the recipient of these decisions, but never a participant in the critical thinking process. The HDC should teach students not only to be critical viewers of individual's lives, but also critical readers of the biographers who are depicting those lives.

15. The HDC is inherently cross-disciplinary, since all the aspects of the biographical subject would be treated simultaneously as the students read about the many dimensions of the person's life. Family, culture, historical context, technological context, and economic context all condition everyone's life. Thus, each life is an opportunity to learn about psychology, history, economics, science, technology, etc. As the HDC progresses, it should be clearer to the students how the different disciplines inform each other within the context of each life studied. Explicit materials can and should be developed to encourage each student to make these connections and discover concrete

cause-and-effect relationships.

16. HDC units should be considered precursors to content units for one reason that might not be obvious to the pedagogue. As everyone knows, the aroma of food cooking tantalizes a hungry person. Restraint in music often sets up a tension, the resolution of which yields immense satisfaction. Mystery and revelation in stage drama are often essential parts of a play's success. The cultivation in agriculture is a necessary precursor to any successful growing season. The same may be true in education. Educators often want to rush to the content of a subject area without cultivating a desire or a perceived need in the mind of the student for the information. The HDC units should be expressly designed around this cultivation process. Accessible stories with challenging mysteries and questions should stimulate a hunger in the students for some form of resolution to the challenges. Developing a working theory of this cultivation process would be a byproduct of the HDC. Open-ended challenges should thus be met with logical reasoned hypotheses that can be tested by library or experimental research. Let the students think before we encourage them to find the answers elsewhere. This thinking process is the type of cultivation we are looking for.

Human Drama from K through 12

One of the greatest challenges and opportunities in designing new components for a college preparatory program is that one is faced with the whole scope of education—from kindergarten through the 12th grade. As an example, we will compare some possibilities that could be developed for the 1st grade, the 8th grade, and the 12th grade.

The first goal of the HDC is to develop a series of units centered on the biographies of individuals in order to: first, show the thinking challenges that they had to overcome and how they did that, second, to extract a set of systems tools that either did implicitly inform or could have informed those thinking processes, and finally, to use these thinking tools to address other situations. The following are examples of possible age-appropriate biographical materials and themes:

1st Grade

George Washington
- *"Father" of our Country (fame)*
- *First President (leadership)*
- *Husband (relationships)*
- *Soldier (learning from mistakes)*
- *Farmer (creativity)*

Descartes
- *Long ago (the nature of history)*
- *Liked to sleep late and stay in bed to think*[67]
- *Soldier*[68]

8th Grade

George Washington
- *Risk taker (What is risk?)*
- *Organizer (weaknesses and strengths)*
- *Leader (threats and opportunities)*
- *Revolutionary War (failures and successes)*
- *Continental Congress (supporters and opponents)*
- *Constitution (fundamental ideas of liberty)*

Descartes
- *Arithmetic (what he knew)*
- *Soldier (environment, strategies and critical thinking)*
- *Thinking (thinking about thinking)*
- *Mathematics Study (the process of learning)*

Faraday
- *Bookbinding (mechanical and chemical processes)*
- *Electricity (What is it?)*
- *Chemistry (What is it?)*
- *The Royal Institution (environmental influence)*

Faulkner
- *Author (What is creative writing?)*

---

[67] Maybe this is not such a good idea to put this idea in their little heads!

[68] This might be a challenge, but try to imagine a reading book that would say, "This is Descartes. See Descartes sleep." – I hope you are chuckling here! Who cares about Dick and Jane anyway? We might as well get some mileage out of their reading exercises. We call this *integrating* the curriculum.

- *Southerner (environmental influence)*

Peter the Great

- *Tsar (the seat of power—different political systems)*
- *Student (the thirst to know)*
- *Leader (styles of leadership)*

12th grade

George Washington

- *Intellect (thinking processes and results)*
- *Diplomat (balancing goals)*
- *President (seat of power—different political systems)*
- *Power Struggles (dealing with opponents, negotiation)*

Descartes

- *Philosopher (supporters and detractors)*
- *Mathematician/Analytical Geometry (challenges)*
- *Scientist (inductive and deductive reasoning)*
- *Church (resource and/or antagonist)*

Faraday

- *Experimentalist (designing experiments, successes, failures)*
- *Empiricist (the value of observation)*
- *Ignorant of Mathematics (overcoming deficiencies)*
- *Intellectual Integrity (How did it influence him?)*
- *Synthesizer (role of critical and creative thinking)*
- *Creativity - Electrical Induction (making the creative leap)*

Faulkner

- *Southern Agrarian (environment)*

- *Humanist (underlying philosophy)*
- *Historian (telling a meaningful story)*
- *Sociologist (the role of human values)*
- *Psychologist (the role of the human psyche)*

Peter the Great

- *Intellect (types of intellectual abilities)*
- *Creativity (something new out of something old)*
- *Thirst (a driving desire)*
- *Vision (the ability to "see beyond")*

Once the biographical materials have been developed, the next step is to glean from them the systems concepts that will help the students in their own cognitive processes. At this point the unit developers might create a set of age-appropriate "universes" that become thinking tools at the various age levels. You will see that, as the student matures, the complexity of the various universes increases and the scope expands. The idea might be, for example, to capture for the student the idea that a triangle only has three sides, so that is all they have to worry about. One does not have to worry about ten things when logic says that there can only be a maximum of three in the universe of possibilities. Once a whole universe has been defined, the number of areas of concern is greatly reduced. Such "wholes" become powerful thinking tools. For example:

1st Grade

- Up – Down – Sideways (motion)
- In – Out
- Me – Others
- Good – Bad
- Family (Father – Mother – Children

    – Grandparents – Cousins)
- Stay – Go
- Walk – Run
- On Foot – Horseback – Boat – Car – Bus – Train – Airplane – Rocket
- Float – Sink

8th Grade
- Up – Down – Sideways – Trajectory (motion)
- Mind – Body – Spirit
- Earth – Sun – Planets – Solar System – Galaxy – Universe
- Social – Antisocial
- Ethical – Unethical
- Linear – Nonlinear
- Internal – External
- Space (1, 2, and 3 dimensions)
- Good – Evil
- Friends – Foes
- Family (Father – Mother – Children – Grandparents – Aunts – Uncles)
- Heavier-Than-Air Flight – Lighter-Than-Air Flight

12th grade
- Up – Down – Sideways – Trajectory – Sinusoidal – Exponential (motion)
- Extended Family (Father – Mother – Children – Grandparents – 1st Cousins – 2nd Cousins – 3rd Cousins Twice Removed)
- Zero-sum games – Non-zero-sum games
- Love – Truth – Beauty

- Empirical – Theoretical
- Physics – Metaphysics
- Ontological – Teleological
- Friends – Foes – Those who look like friends but are foes – Those who look like foes but are friends
- Liars – Honest Folks – Equivocators – Agnostics – Prophets – Scaredy-cats
- Space – Time
- Absolute – Relative
- Theme – Plot – Characters – Setting
- Dynamic – Static
- Rational – Irrational
- Stochastic – Deterministic
- Linear – Geometric – Exponential
- Science – Math – Literature – Art – Humanities
- Prose – Poetry
- Science – Engineering – Technology
- Executive – Judicial – Legislative
- Planning – Leading – Organizing – Controlling
- Inputs – Processes – Sensors – Standards – Comparators – Correctors – Outputs (Control Loop)
- First-Order – Second-Order – Third-Order – Etc.
- War – Peace – Tension – Conflict – Resolution – Dissolution
- The Cell (James Greer Miller)
  - Boundary
  - Reproducer
  - Energy/Matter
    - Distributor
    - Converter
    - Producer

- Storage
- Extruder
- Utilizer
- Information
  - Decoder
  - Memory
  - Transmitter
  - Utilizer

The idea is that the systems universes become successively more complex yet build on previous systems, so that the curriculum becomes more integrated and cumulative. Our goal is to be able to see the analogy of a system operating in one setting so that we can apply it to another setting. We call this process *mapping*, and in order to do this we often have to use a more abstract language to refer to the system components than would be used in the discipline from which the system originates. This language, as we have seen previously, is called a *meta-language*. You can see this operative above in the language used to describe the components of a cell. James Greer Miller wrote a groundbreaking application of systems thinking in his massive work entitled *Living Systems*.[69] In this work he shows that by creating a broad enough meta-language for the components of a cell, he can show through a process of mapping, how these same elements operate in biological organs, organisms, groups, organizations, societies, and supranational systems. In this context all of these living systems would be seen to be *isomorphic*—having the same form. Some systems are easily mapped from one to another. Others require a subtle meta-language to reveal the relationships. As students move through the curriculum, they become more and more sophisticated in their ability to see the

---

[69]   James Greer Miller, *Living Systems* (McGraw-Hill, 1978), 1102 pp.

elements, attributes, and relations of the components of a system, creating a versatile meta-language and using it to identify isomorphic systems.

Another example of this approach might be the system Executive-Judiciary-Legislative. We will all recognize this system as our form of government with the inherent checks and balances this system creates. The challenge is to see the functionality of each branch and create a more abstract language that reflects this functionality. The next systems question one might ask is whether these three branches represent some kind of universe of possibilities. If indeed this is the case, then we are in a good position to look for other systems that utilize this same form of "command and control." For example, in a family, who is acting as a representative of each branch? Where are the checks and balances? It is certainly different for each family of each student. To make this kind of assessment the student must use all the forms of thinking.

The universes described above represent important thinking tools that show the student where to look for components of the critical thinking process. Once these universes have been identified by the unit developers, they can be used as a guide for looking at biographical materials that would allow the student to expose these systems and how they are working, not only in the lives of the subjects, but also in the lives of the students, as well as in the other pedagogical content of the curriculum.

As is evident from the above sketch, it is possible to accomplish a number of tasks by the design of the curriculum. Here we are integrating across the grade levels by treating the same personalities several times, each time at a deeper and more complex level. In each case, the systems tools that would be drawn out of student discussions would be successively more complex and give the students the opportunity to analyze the characters and their thinking processes, use their own creative thinking to create the systems metalanguages that would allow the possibility for relating systems operative in one life to other situations, and finally to use critical thinking to do the mapping. (Actually, all three types of thinking overlap continuously.)

Conclusion

Human Drama Across the Curriculum is a bold approach to engage both students and teachers in the same processes that take place every moment of every day in every corner of the earth as individuals are confronted with challenges that must be recognized, addressed, and ultimately met. It is this inherent ability to engage and integrate that makes HDAC a compelling addition to any school or liberal arts college curriculum. Its focus on thinking and problem solving makes it an ideal complement to any curriculum content for school students who are college bound or liberal arts students who are moving toward a career in the professions. The skills developed are precisely the skills that are needed for success in business school, law school, medical school or seminary as well as for any subsequent career path.

For further information on curriculum development and potential funding please contact:

The Denver Institute for Integrative Studies
14 Inverness Drive Ease, Suite F-160
Englewood, CO 80112
(303) 708-1629

Acknowledgements

This project arose out of an effort by Bob Muldoon and myself to develop an educational proposal for the Athens Academy in Athens, Georgia. Primarily I would like to offer my sincerest thanks to Bob who established the initial contact with the Academy and both encouraged and contributed to the original proposal. His influence is still evident in the present work. I would also like to thank the Athens Academy for their encouragement and consideration of the original proposal. Because this is a systems proposal, I should mention the great debt I owe to John C. Griffiths (deceased), a professor of mine at Penn State, who introduced me to the systems community and the whole corpus of systems thinking. Without that insight, the connections made here would not have been possible.

I should also acknowledge my appreciation for the two years I spent at Benedict College in Columbia, South Carolina and the opportunity to stretch into academic areas that would not have been available to me elsewhere. The laboratory experience alluded to in the text concerning the making of iron was highly formative in my understanding of some approaches to teaching and the thinking processes. I would also like to thank Dr. John R. Carpenter, my professor in Geology at the University of South Carolina and a teacher committed to the development of teachers as founder of the University of South Carolina Center for Science Education.

It was my work in its Summer Science Institute that offered me the opportunity to develop the "water cycle" lab mentioned in the text. As my master's degree advisor, he was always a model of intellectual thirst and integrity.

I would be remiss in not generally acknowledging all my teachers through the years who offered me their best efforts as they understood them and gave of their lives that others and I might learn and grow into productive and happy people. I went to high school at Aiken Senior High in Aiken, South Carolina. Mrs. Bobo stands out as a monument to intellectual discipline. I majored in chemistry at the University of the South in Sewanee, Tennessee and was blessed by demanding professors such as Drs. David Camp, Jim Lowe, Bill Gunther, and Felder Dorn. I managed the distinction of being third in my graduating class in chemistry—and last. They all were patient with me, and there is no part of my intellectual journey that has not been informed by their efforts. I spent two and a half years in a PhD program in Geochemistry in the Department of Geosciences at Penn State before I moved to Mineral Economics. I would like to offer my sincere thanks and gratitude to Dr. Derrill Kerrick who had to put up with my own intellectual struggle and, in the process, offered me an invaluable experience in pure scientific investigation. It is so hard when a graduate student abandons one program for another, and advisors must ruminate over the reasons and the lost effort. I would like to assure him that the fruits of that experience are being manifest every day in my life, and I will always be eternally grateful to him. Derrill, I owe you. At the end of this string of dedicated professionals who have influenced me would be my PhD dissertation advisor, John Tilton, in the Department of Mineral Economics at Penn State. The process of immersing oneself in a narrow topic to become an "expert" is such a fundamental aspect of learning without which, I dare say, I could not have appreciated the joy of true discovery and creative thinking. That certainly is not the only way, but it is an important one. I thank him deeply for the opportunity to have that experience.

Finally, the love and support I have received from my mother and father, Gertrude and Bob Fletcher, and my sister Penny throughout my life are precious reminders of the power of environment in the formation if thinking processes and the thirst to know. Of course I offer, especially to Bob Muldoon, the requisite disclaimer—much of the good stuff in this proposal I owe to others—all the errors or inadequate thinking are of my own doing.

About the Author

Jonathan Fletcher was born nine months after his father was discharged from the US Army Air Corps in January of 1946—a quintessential baby boomer. He grew up in Aiken, South Carolina, went to the University of the South (Sewanee), the University of South Carolina, and Penn State. He has taught ninth grade physical science and both undergraduate and graduate courses in geology, chemistry and mineral economics, as well as professional courses in management, and petroleum technology. He lives in Littleton, Colorado and is currently the director of the Denver Institute for Integrative Studies and is involved in a number of consulting relationships related to technological and managerial budgeting and planning. He is also the author of *The Quiz: On the Nature of the Incarnation of Jesus Christ* (St Maximus Scriptorium, 2012).

www.ingramcontent.com/pod-product-compliance
Lightning Source LLC
Chambersburg PA
CBHW032045040426
42449CB00007B/996